MARCO  POLO

SOUTH AFR ICA

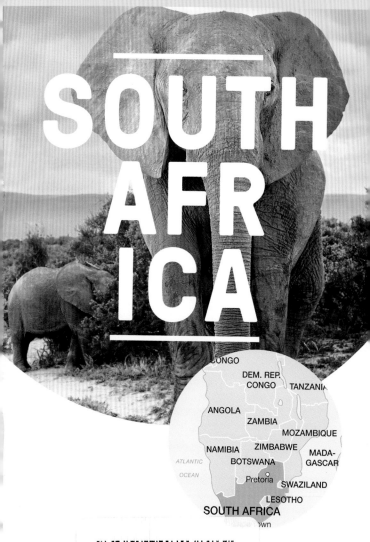

CONGO
DEM. REP. CONGO TANZANIA
ANGOLA
ZAMBIA
MOZAMBIQUE
NAMIBIA ZIMBABWE MADA-GASCAR
BOTSWANA
ATLANTIC OCEAN
Pretoria
SWAZILAND
LESOTHO
SOUTH AFRICA
...own

T0150578

www.marco-polo.com

GET MORE OUT OF YOUR MARCO POLO GUIDE

IT'S AS SIMPLE AS THIS

1 go.marco-polo.com/saf

2 download and discover

GO!

WORKS OFFLINE!

SYMBOLS

INSIDER TIP	Insider Tip
★	Highlight
●●●●	Best of...
☼	Scenic view
⊘	Responsible travel: for ecological or fair trade aspects
(*)	Telephone numbers that are not toll-free

HOTELS

Expensive	over 1540 rand
Moderate	925–1540 rand
Budget	under 925 rand

Prices per night for two people in a double room with breakfast

RESTAURANTS

Expensive	over 460 rand
Moderate	230–460 rand
Budget	under 230 rand

Prices for a meal with starter, main course and dessert

DID YOU KNOW?
Tineline → p. 14
Burn, Baby ,Burn! → p. 23
Local specialities → p. 28
Step into the unknown
→ p. 45
For film buffs → p. 56
For bookworms → p. 62
By luxury train through South
Africa → p. 109
National holidays → p. 119
Budgeting → p. 124
Currency Converter → p. 125
Weather → p. 126

MAPS IN THE GUIDEBOOK
(130 A1) Page numbers and
coordinates refer to the road
atlas
(0) Site/address located off
the map
Coordinates are also given for
places that are not marked
on the road atlas
Map of Johannesburg on p.
138/139

(*◫ A–B 2–3*) refers to the
removable pull-out map
(*◫ a–b 2–3*) refers to the in-
sert map on te pull-out map

INSIDE FRONT COVER:
The best Highlights

INSIDE BACK COVER:
Map of Cape Town (U A1)

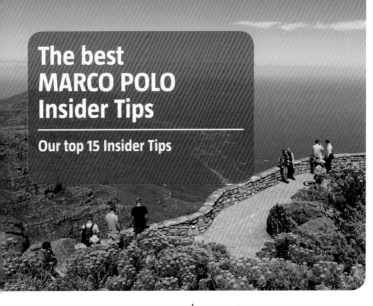

The best MARCO POLO Insider Tips

Our top 15 Insider Tips

INSIDER TIP **The name says it all**
Located high above Wilderness' 5 km (3 mile) stretch of pristine beach is the boutique hotel *Views*. This ocean retreat resembles one gigantic aquarium inside where guests can decide if they want to get wet → **p. 36**

INSIDER TIP **Half-price sundowners**
Take advantage of the Table Mountain special – cable car rides are only half price at sunset in the summer months (photo above) → **p. 54**

INSIDER TIP **Sea view**
Get some of the best Indian Ocean views at the *African Perfection* B & B in the world famous surfers' paradise of Jeffrey's Bay. Make sure that you ask for the corner guest bedroom on the first floor → **p. 49**

INSIDER TIP **In vino veritas**
Doolhof wine estate near Paarl produces excellent wines and visitors can also stay over in the manor house → **p. 63**

INSIDER TIP **Food at Cleopatra's**
After a hike in Drakensberg Mountains, you'll appreciate a seat at a finely laid table, particularly if you are served the delightful menu at the *Cleopatra Mountain Farmhouse* → **p. 79**

INSIDER TIP **By bike in the township**
Learn Soweto's cool "shake, grip thumbs and shake again" handshake on a bike tour through Soweto → **p. 85**

INSIDER TIP **Bush whisper**
No need to worry about catching malaria at the *Madikwe Game Reserve* in the north on the border to Botswana. Just relax in one of its 20 secluded lodges and watch out for the big five passing by (photo right) → **p. 93**

INSIDER TIP **Brakes check**
It's downhill virtually all of the way from Tafelberg - a challenge for any mountain biker → **p. 111**

INSIDER TIP **A powerhouse stay**
The old power station on Knysna lagoon has recently been converted into the *Turbine Hotel*. The boutique hotel is an eclectic mix of industrial design and art – its old industrial machinery is under heritage protection → p. 43

INSIDER TIP **No expense spared**
Bree Street is the coolest place to shop in the whole of Cape Town where you can find luxury items for back home → p. 55

INSIDER TIP **Diggin' it**
Guests to the *Royal Hotel* in Pilgrim's Rest feel like the discoverers of the gold rush over 100 years ago – with just a touch of added comfort → p. 92

INSIDER TIP **Shaken and stirred**
The new generation of speciality cocktails mixed at *Sin & Taxes* in Johannesburg are low in sugar and crafted with homemade ingredients → p. 86

INSIDER TIP **Join the BBQ**
You need a large appetite and a love of fish to visit the beachside *Strandloper* restaurant in Langebaan where freshly caught fish and sea food are thrown straight on the beach barbecue → p. 46

INSIDER TIP **Time machine**
Not sure which hotel to stay at during your trip to the Karoo? Simply stroll down the main street in Cradock lined with *Tuishuise* and choose one of the Victorian houses → p. 38

INSIDER TIP **Fisherman's retreat**
A nondescript shack from the outside, yet the inside of *Panama Jacks* could be the setting for the memoirs of many sailors in Cape Town's industrial port and serves authentic sea food → p. 55

BEST OF...

FOR FREE

● *Glistening diamonds*
Documenting the exciting era of the diamond rush is the *Big Hole and Kimberley Mine Museum*. Whereas there is an admission charge for the former, entrance to the museum is free. Several thousand genuine diamonds can be viewed in the *diamond vault* → p. 40

● *Giants of the deep*
The small coastal town of *Hermanus* is renowned as a whale watching venue. Every year between June and December hundreds of whales from the Antarctic converge in the bay and can be viewed from the shore — a very special sight — and it's free (photo) → p. 60

● *Climb up Table Mountain*
It may prove strenuous along the way but the *Platteklip Gorge* is one of the most popular hiking routes on the Tafelberg and well worth the one-hour uphill trek. Once at the top, the whole of Cape Town stands below you. And you can save the price of a cable car ride for a drink at the summit → p. 54

● *Priceless*
The *Tatham Art Gallery* in Pietermaritzburg displays some excellent contemporary South African and international art. Admission is free of charge and on Wednesdays there is the added bonus of a concert → p. 78

● *A stroller's paradise*
Durban's beach promenade is popular with families, surfers, sport enthusiasts and couples. In other words, just about everyone. At the top of the *Golden Mile* you can walk past the aquariums of *Ushaka Marine World* without having to pay the admission price → p. 73

● *A free Garden of Eden*
Unlike Adam and Eva, you will not have a high price to pay to enjoy the Garden Route Botanical Garden – admission is free to visitors → p. 34

◖◗●● Dots in guidebook refer to "Best of..." tips

ONLY IN SOUTH AFRICA
Unique experiences

● *Wine hopping*

A strict alcohol limit wards off drivers from wine-tasting at the hundreds of vineyards around Stellenbosch. With the *Vine Hopper* wine tour, you can experience this region and taste its fantastic wines by way of a hop on-hop off service! → p. 65

● *The perfect wave*

Surfers rate the small town of *Jeffrey's Bay* near Port Elizabeth as the best surf spot on the African continent. Here they can catch the perfect wave at the Super Tubes break (photo) → p. 49

● *Nothing paltry about this poultry*

South Africans are known for their love of meat, especially big steaks prepared on a *braai*. For the more health conscious, ostrich meat is becoming increasingly popular – the meat is tasty but low in fat and cholesterol. Visit the *Cango Ostrich Farm* in Oudtshoorn to learn more → p. 36

● *A sunset to remember*

Sundowners are an institution in South Africa so what better place to enjoy yours than on top of the *Franschhoek Pass.* With views across the valley almost as far as Cape Town and a bottle of your favourite regional wine in hand – life is beautiful → p. 58

● *A journey through time*

The *Basotho Cultural Village* in the Free State will give you first-hand insights into how the Basotho have lived for centuries. The mountains that separate South Africa from Lesotho are their home and here visitors get to meet the chief, try the home brew and make the acquaintance of a sangoma → p. 70

● *Under the old oak trees*

Dorp Street in Stellenbosch takes you back in time to how South Africa was in the first decades after the Cape was colonised. The oaks in this street are listed and carry special significance for the town's student population – superstition has it that if an acorn falls on your head you will pass your exams → p. 64

ONLY IN

BEST OF...

● **Shop till you drop**
More people visit the *Victoria & Alfred (V & A for short) Waterfront* in Cape Town than Table Mountain or the pyramids in Egypt. This shopping emporium encompasses several buildings and is part of a working harbour (photo) → p. 54

● **Underwater world**
Visitors to the *Ushaka Marine World* in Durban can see all types of sea animals in action and up close while staying warm and dry → p. 74

● **Bastion of history**
The *Castle of Good Hope* is South Africa's oldest building. Today it is home to several interesting museums – and a few ghosts from days gone by → p. 52

● **A good vintage**
Wine tasting is always a good way to while away the time when it rains. A good option is the Constantia Wine Route only 20 minutes from central Cape Town with some excellent estates like *Groot Constantia* which is also the oldest of its kind in Africa → p. 53

● **World Heritage site**
Located 40km (25mi) from Johannesburg is the *Cradle of Humankind,* a network of sandstone caves in which the fossilised remains of the hominids that roamed Africa several million years ago have been found. The homo naledi is humankind's newest ancestor → p. 87

● **Franschhoek Motor Museum**
More than 200 cars and motorbikes covering a century of motor vehicle history make this collection on the *L'Ormarins* wine estate one of a kind in South Africa → p. 58

RAIN

RELAX AND CHILL OUT
Take it easy and spoil yourself

CHILL OUT

● *Rejuvenating winery*

This is relaxation: drive out of Cape Town for 25 minutes, rip your clothes off and let yourself be rubbed with coffee and mint in the spa of the beautiful *Steenberg Country Hotel*. The massages are also available for couples → **p. 57**

● *Mountain escape*

If you want to get away from it all and relax then head to the *Homtini Guest Farm* in the Outeniqua Mountains near Knysna. Pamper body and mind with an aromatherapy massage or enjoy some locally farmed food for the soul with a relaxing picnic in the wild → **p. 43**

● *City getaway*

The *One & Only Hotel* is a resort and spa right in middle of Cape Town's V & A Waterfront that offers a varied spa programme with the emphasis on products and plants sourced from Africa. Perfect haven of calm amid the hustle and bustle of the city → **p. 56**

● *On the water's edge*

Water has a very therapeutic role to play in our lives and this fact had a role to play when the architects of *Moyo uShaka* in Durban built a bar at the end of a disused pier, the perfect spot to enjoy that sundowner (photo) → **p. 75**

● *Traditional healing*

The *Fordoun Hotel & Spa* in KwaZulu-Natal is a resort with a difference. Its owner John collaborated with African traditional healer Dr Elliot Ndlovu to develop treatments and products using indigenous healing plants and age-old local recipes → **p. 78**

● *Beachside retreat*

Sun, wooden decks and cocktails in front of luxurious ocean yachts – the *Grand Café & Beach* is part of Cape Town's waterfront and guarantees the perfect holiday feeling → **p. 54**

INTRODUCTION

DISCOVER
SOUTH AFRICA!

First things first: South Africa cannot be summed up in just one sentence. *Its diversity is an adventure* and the country's astounding variety is what grabs you and won't let go. Visitors often leave with smiles on their faces, inspired by their wealth of experiences and with travel stories to share with anyone willing to listen back home. Nelson Mandela, the father of South Africa's relatively new democracy and its first State President, often spoke of his *rainbow nation* – although it glosses over some of the country's serious issues, the phrase encapsulates the coming-together of colours to create a magnificent spectrum.

The diversity is reflected in its various official languages: South Africa has eleven in total: Zulu, Xhosa, Afrikaans, Northern Sotho, Sesotho, Tswana, Tsonga, Swati, Ndebele, Venda and English not to mention its many unofficial languages and dialects. Indeed it is as complicated as it sounds. Every South African can speak at least five of the eleven languages, even if the knowledge is limited to singing along to the country's national anthem "Nkosi Sikelel' iAfrika". Rated as one of the *world's most evocative anthems*, it often leaves sport stadium spectators with goose bumps when it is sung by the crowd. If you want to collect a few bonus points with locals while on your

Chatting, browsing, shooping – organic market in the Old Biscuit Mill in Cape Town

journeys around the country, besides greeting with the obligatory "Howzit?", you can also say "Sawubona!" (in Zulu) or "Dumelang!" (in Tswana) depending on the region you are visiting. *Speaking of travelling, South Africa offers excellent transport possibilities* whether you choose to go from north to south, east to west or vice versa be it by plane (relatively inexpensive), luxury train (slow paced and comfortable) or road trip by motorbike or car. The best time to visit South Africa is between October and April. The seasons in the southern hemisphere are exactly opposite to those in Europe so when the weather turns grey, wet and dreary back home,

> **South Africans always like a chat**

100 BC
The Khoisan people migrated to the south of the continent from central Africa

600 AD
The first Bantu tribes settled on the east coast of South Africa

1488
Bartholomew Diaz circumnavigated the Cape of Good Hope

1652
First white settlers under Jan van Riebeeck founded a supply station at the Cape

1658
Arrival of Asian and African slaves

it becomes nice and warm in South Africa. It's not a bad idea to roughly plan what you want to see and do – preferably while drinking a glass of South African *wine* – before setting off on your journey. The choice of places to visit is staggering and the distances between them are vast. A more relaxing alternative would be to take full advantage of the full ninety days available to UK tourists without needing a visa.

Many cultures – lots of fun

The classic of all *road trips* takes you from Johannesburg to Cape Town through the semidesert of Karoo and covers a vast 1400 km/870 miles. Coastal enthusiasts can look forward to 3000 km/1860 miles of road along the Atlantic and Indian Ocean. Wildlife watching in one of the country's national parks also requires time and patience. The Kruger Park has a surface area the size of Wales and it can take hours to travel just a few dozen miles from one camp to the next when the road is blocked by *wild animals for photo shooting*. The old saying "There is no hurry in Africa" also applies in the continent's south. What hectic Europeans refer to as slow is in fact the normal pace of most South Africans and as soon as you adapt to it, you will experience some unique moments whether it be the sun on your skin, the smile of a passer-by or a local who will spontaneously ask "How are you?". In virtually every situation – except when an elephant is chasing your car in torrential rain – South Africans will strike up a conversation. These greetings are a way of uniting all the country's ethnicities whose cultures are so very different.

1688 Arrival of the French Huguenots

1795 British occupation of the Cape

1814 Boer rebellion against British rule

1835 The Boers began their Great Trek north

1838 Battle of Blood River between Boers and Zulus

1867 Discovery of first diamond

1886 Founding of the city of Johannesburg

To name just a few of these groups in non-chronological order: although the *Ndebele* is the smallest ethnic group, their colourful wall paintings and intricate bead necklaces have made them the South African stereotype similar to Londoners are for England. The second most photographed group are the *proud Zulus* from the north-east. Nine million of South Africa's total population (54 million) are Zulus. They wear strips of hide for adornment, believe in ancestor spirits who have the power to intervene in people's destiny and honour King Shaka, who founded this tribe in the early 19th century. The capital of the Kwa-Zulu Natal province is Durban which has *more overseas Indians* than any other city outside India; one quarter of the city's population has Indian origins. Durban becomes extremely overcrowded during the Christmas and Easter holidays; its tropical climate attracts tens of thousands of tourists to the warm ocean. The regions in the North and Eastern Cape in the Karoo semidesert reveal a completely different landscape which is arid, barren and *vast* with deep-blue skies where the sun burns down during the day and astronomers come for the spectacular stars at night. This unpopulated region has almost no light pollution and the stars literally light up the night sky.

A long way towards freedom

In the Free State – as in the Northern provinces – it rains only in summer when everything seems to turn green overnight. In the western Namaqualand on the Atlantic coast, the countryside transforms into *a sea of wild flowers* each year from August to October – a truly unbelievable sight. Most of this region's inhabitants are referred to as *Coloureds*, ancestors of the Bushmen, the politically correct term being Khoisan. As a result of South Africa's apartheid history, most of the Coloureds work on farms if they are fortunate enough to have a job. Most speak Afrikaans just like the farmers who today own the land of their ancestors. From 1835, the first European settlers (mainly from Holland and Germany) intrepidly emigrated from the Cape with their oxen-pulled carts settling inland in the great vast open plains. They were strong, hardened farmers and the Afrikaans word for them is *Boer*, still used to describe the descendants of these settlers. They are a nature-loving, conservative and friendly group of people holding strong family values and easily recognisable for their children who walk around barefoot. During the apartheid era, the South African Boer government enforced

1910
Merger between British colonies and Boer republic into the South African Union

1948
Apartheid became legislation

1960
Pass law uprisings, 60 dead in Sharpeville

1961
Withdrawal from the Commonwealth

1976
Pupil unrest in Soweto

1990
Activist Nelson Mandela released

A Zulu village in the Kwazulu-Natal province behind the picturesque backdrop of the Drakensberg

a strict policy of segregation. Non-white citizens were discriminated against, exploited and the country became increasingly isolated for its apartheid policies. International pressure and the struggle for freedom organised by today's ruling party, the ANC, eventually caused the system to be abolished. *Nelson Mandela* then became the first democratically elected president. More than twenty years after the country's struggle for freedom, South Africa is still try-

The rainbow has to prove itself

ing to find its own identity. Yet every culture has retained its own unique *friendly and welcoming attitude* displaying humour, optimism and a laid-back manner. An appealing mixture whose charm won't let go of you.

1994
Nelson Mandela voted as president in first free democratic elections

2001
South Africa's Peace and Reconciliation Commission submitted its report

2009
Jacob Zuma became South Africa's fourth president since full democracy

2010
South Africa became the first African country to host the World Cup

5 Dec 2013
Nelson Mandela dies aged 95

2015
New human species found in South Africa: Homo naledi

WHAT'S HOT

1 Secret sunrise

Rise and Shine Join the crowds of partying early birds to celebrate the start of the day with *Secret Sunrise.* South Africans have always loved waking up early and have now started this movement which invites groups of people to venues, kept a secret until shortly before the dancing to celebrate the sunrise. There is no fighting and no disturbing neighbours because each person is given their own set of headphones. *Secret Sunrise Events* are organised in Cape Town, Johannesburg and Durban. *www.secret sunrise.com*

Identity in Art

2

Art If you have any spare cash going, then visit some of the cities' art galleries because (South) African art is in vogue. Your money probably won't stretch to an original from the famous artist William Kentridge or the sculptures by Norman Catherine (photo) yet luckily there are other young contemporary artists on display at the *Everard Read Gallery (www.everard-read. co.za)* in Johannesburg or the *Stevenson Gallery* in Cape Town *(www.stevenson.info)*.

3 Wild food foraging

Edible landscapes Anyone can go into a restaurant, call the waiter and order food. It's far more fun to search for food yourself, learning where to find the ingredients which make up the fantastic Cape cuisine. At *Wild Food Foraging* the inspiring Roushanna Gray takes you on an adventure to find food in the ground and on the beach *(www. veldandsea.com)*. The urban hunter and gatherer Charles Standing cooperates with the *Table Bay Hotel* (photo) in Cape Town for his tours to conjure up delicious menus *(www. theurbanhuntergatherer.com)*.

An audience of laughter

Live is live   Dressed in costumes and bow ties, they sing about racism, poke fun at dialects in dialect and are not afraid to pack a punch – South African comedians like to put on a good performance. An evening in the *Cape Town Comedy Club (The Pumphouse | V&A Waterfront | www.capetowncomedy.com)* is just as informative as watching the news but far funnier. An alternative venue with an weekly open mic session is the *Comedy on a Roll (Wed from 9pm)* at the *Obviouzly Armchair Backpackers & Pub (135 Lower Main Road | Observatory)* (photo). Also check out the *POPArt Theatre (286 Fox Street | Maboneng | www.popartcentre.co.za)* in Johannesburg!

Hipster city

Function follows form   Ever since Cape Town was officially named as the World Design Capital in 2014, the city has embraced contemporary design. Everything from a tooth brush holder to a night lamp – the range of cleverly designed, quirky and cool items is staggering. The best place to start hunting is along Loop Street at *Stable Design Emporium (www.stable.org.za)* or in the gentrification district of Woodstock, home to hip furniture in *Gregor Jenkin Studio (1 Argyle Street | www.gregorjenkin.com)*. ALeft and right of the Old Biscuit Mill (photo) along Albert Road also offers excellent places to browse around. Don't spend too long there or else you will miss your reservation at the *Pot Luck Club (375 Albert Road | tel. 02 14 47 08 04 | www.thepotluckclub.co.za | Moderate)* which serves the perfectly designed tapas on the top floor of this former silo.

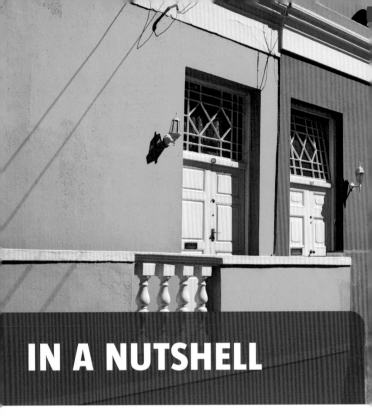

IN A NUTSHELL

CASTING LONG SHADOWS

Eish! This Zulu term is used to express all types of exasperation, disbelief or sadness and is the perfect expression to sum up the apartheid in one word. With World War II in Europe barely over, the Boer Government in South Africa had nothing better to do than segregate the black from the white people by law. Approximately three quarters of the population were forced to relocate to the countryside in cramped conditions in so-called *Bantustans,* they could not sit on the same park benches never mind go to the same schools as their white counterparts and mixed-race relationships were taboo. The apartheid state classified all South Africans into one of four racial groups: white, Indian, *coloured* and black – the darker the skin, the fewer rights they had. One particularly perfidious act was the so-called "pencil test" performed by the authorities. If the pencil stuck when the person shook his head, the person was considered black, if it fell out, he was classified as *coloured.* If the pencil did not stay in the person's hair at all, then the person "passed" the test as white. Some families were even split apart as a result of this test. This unfair system goes deep into the country's psyche and race debates are a mine field and should only be entered by experts on this subject.

TATA MADIBA

He was the face of South Africa - this affectionately loved and honoured man

Red bush and diamonds, Nelson Mandela and the Big Five: understand how South Africa lives and breathes

was deeply mourned throughout the nation. When Nelson Rolihlahla Mandela died on December 5 2013, the rainbow nation became a reality. People from diverse ethnic groups held each other in their arms, sang together at bus stops and were convinced to do better in the future in his honour. Known affectionately by his clan's name Madiba, Mandela served 27 years in prison for this moment of reconciliation. His superhuman ability to forgive and his charisma saved South Africa from civil war while the apartheid

system turned into a democracy. He was released in 1990 and was jointly awarded the Noble Peace Prize with the last white president of the country, Frederik Willem de Klerk. He was elected president in 1994 for just one term. Nelson Mandela knew that South Africa had to find a way forward without him.

EACH TO HIS OWN SPORT

Let me look at you and I'll tell you what sport you like. Although it sounds like a poor chat-up line, there is much truth in this saying. Nelson Mandela deliberately wore a rugby shirt of the South African national team, the Springboks, at the 1995 Rugby World Cup and rejoiced in the team's victory. This was seen throughout the world as a gesture in reconciliation because rugby is tradi-

which meant football became the sport of the black people and the townships hosted legendary tournaments. Even when the national team *(Bafana Bafana)* is performing badly, their fans still adore them and try to blow the ball into the goal with their famous vuvuzelas. If you're interested in sport, a ticket to

Ready for kick-off in the Cape Town stadium: only the rugby players are missing

tionally a white-man's sport in South Africa, introduced by the Boers and the British. Under apartheid, rugby was also segregated and prevented talented black players from being promoted and even today professional rugby continues to be predominately white. Amid the run-up to the 2015 Rugby World Cup in England, much heated discussion centred on the "pigment quote" which unfortunately "tackled" the problem at the wrong end and was eventually rejected.

The opposite is true as far as football is concerned – the majority of players and fans are black. Mixed-race teams were forbidden during the apartheid

the Soweto derby between the Orlando Pirates and Kaizer Chiefs is a must on your to-do list.

Cricket is also the second most popular sport in South Africa and is the only sport in the country to feature in the top 2 sports of all race groups. Established by the British, cricket is popular among the country's English-speaking as well as Asian and Indian community. The country has gradually advanced to one of the world's leading cricket nations. A fact of interest: the national team is nicknamed *Proteas* after South Africa's national flower.

RED BUSH

When Annette and Chris du Plessis take their guests on safari tours, they are invited to bring along a magnifying glass instead of a pair of binoculars. The red bush plant, or *Rooibos* as it is known in Afrikaans, is the species under observation on these tours and your guide Chris explains the benefits of this particular beverage: no caffeine, plenty of antioxidants, iron and zinc. Rooibos tea is the ultimate in healthy brews and tastes delicious which is why it is now consumed in many countries. Demand could exceed supply seen as the red bush plant only grows in the Cederberg mountains and is part of the fynbos family – the name of the unique natural vegetation located on the Western Cape. Guests learn about these aspects and more besides on the tea plantation farm belonging to Annette and Chris du Plessis and are invited on tours through rooibos landscape *(www.elandsberg. co.za | see p. 104)*. The Khoisan people were the first to make tea from this aromatic plant long before European botanists caught wind of this special team and established rooibos farms in the region. Today there is a wide range of aromatic and healthy rooibos products, so many that you may not have enough room left in your suitcase after visiting Clanwilliam: lotions, shower gels, soaps, lemonades or recipe books are all available to buy. All low-caffeine, hot beverage junkies should try the *Red Cappuccino,* the hipster among the rooibos teas.

BLING, BLING!

When treasure hunters go diving for treasure, they pull on their wetsuits, take out their underwater suction pipes and head out to sea. A similar procedure is followed by the diamond divers of Port Nolloth. Although a seemingly nondescript place, this northwest coastal resort (just south of the Namibia border) has vast treasures underneath the seabed: diamonds to be precise which were swept over millions of years to the Atlantic ocean floor off the coast of Port Nolloth. These are so-called "conflict-free" diamonds and therefore have become

BURN, BABY ,BURN!

The Karoo semidesert is desolate in April, a dusty outcrop, hot during the day and freezing cold at night. A stalking ground for hungry coyotes. Probably not your idea of a great week? But wait a minute, the desert has become a gathering for mermaids, artists, men from Mars, rockers, dancers and other creative minds. A mixture of utopia and Mad Max where crowds flock in thousands with their friends and on their far-out vehicles. This community creates an alternative world free of money where everyone is invited to contribute their creativity for the entertainment or food, one of the principles if you want to take part. The festival is called *Afrika Burn* and was inspired by *Burning Man* in Nevada, USA. The desert is turned into a fantasy city, performances are held in the shadows of gigantic works of art and guests dance the nights away. When it's over, the party people leave in the same way they came. The artworks are either burned or taken away – and guests are left with their memories. *www.afrikaburn.com*

extremely precious. Companies can buy diving licenses for the area and diamond divers then swim down to the ocean bed and use large suction pipes to pump up the sand and gravel. Any diamond found here must be declared to a state-controlled authority. The prices for the stones are set by the international market and theft is punished.

Tourists have also recently joined in the diamond hunting fun. You need to be a strong swimmer though to tackle the sea around the Benguela Current - often compared to a gigantic spinning washing machine – and have the right amount of cash on hand. *Benguela Diamonds (www.bengueladiamonds.com)* will take guests down to the seabed for around 16,000 dollars. However it goes without saying that what you find must be paid for.

B ABYLONIAN

Mlungu – in English this means white man or woman. This is one of the words you will certainly hear on a cross-country road trip. The cool response would be to reply with *Yebo!,* the friendly exclamation to show agreement or approval in Zulu. Other insider vocabulary includes *Howzit?* used to inquire about a person's health and wellbeing. If the waiter says he's coming *now,* it could take a few hours. The chances are better if he says *now now* and you've hit the jackpot if you hear *just now.* If an Afrikaans-speaking person likes something, he will refer to it as *lekker.* Take a tour through the township and you will be greeted by locals on all corners with a *Sharp!* and a thumbs-up. In contrast *Eish!* is used to complain about a flat tyre or if you've missed your plane. *Mzanzi* stands for South Africa. And if you hear the word *robots* when someone describes the way somewhere, don't worry South Africa is

not so technologically advanced, they are simply referring to the good old traffic lights.

A TTENTION!

The golden rule of safety in notorious South Africa is "Just don't be stupid". Despite the horror stories which circulate about tourists being the victims of crime, most visitors manage to get through an entire holiday or longer stay without any unpleasant experiences. As long as you always have in the back of your mind that there is a huge gap between the rich and the poor and that many criminals try their luck because they have nothing to lose. Remember to securely fasten your bags in public, leave any valuable jewellery and electronic items back in the hotel and make sure you don't stray off the beaten tourist tracks – the same rules apply as in all other countries. Never let a stranger help you at a cash machine, regardless of how confusing the situation may appear and never leave your handbag on the passenger seat. In larger cities such as Cape Town and Johannesburg, if you notice that another car has been tailing you for some time, drive around the block again or head to the nearest petrol station or police station.

W ILD THINGS

What do lions, leopards, elephants, rhinos and buffalos have in common? They are all among the *Big Five,* the list of animals every wildlife lover wants to spot and take photos of on safari in order to show off to their friends back home. South Africa has many state-owned and private parks to choose from where you can drive around in your own vehicle – it is of course strictly forbidden to get out during the drive – or accompanied by rangers who are trained to spot the mere glance of a gazelle's tail hiding

A zebra crossing in the Madikwe Game Reserve

behind a bush. The best time of the day for the *game drives* are early morning or just before sunset. The private lodges often pack their open-top jeeps with snacks and drinks to serve to their guests. Wildlife protection is expensive which is why private parks generally have more luxurious accommodation to justify the high prices. South Africa has always been exemplary when it comes to nature conservation and this policy also forms part of its constitution. In the past few years cross-border Transfrontier Parks have been established between South Africa and Namibia and between South Africa, Zimbabwe and Mozambique.

EMPTY STOMACHS – HELPING HANDS

You cannot overlook the fact that poverty is part of everyday life in South Africa. The injustices of the past are one reason but a serious lack of jobs is another. The official unemployment rate is around 30 percent but head out to the townships and it feels like every second person is struggling to feed his family. However tourists should resist the temptation of handing out bank notes. It makes more sense to visit one of the country's excellent aid projects and give them a long-term donation. Another way of offering help is to buy a souvenir from the many street dealers. Beggars on the streets usually appreciate a sandwich or second-hand clothing rather than a few coins. One traditional and caring, if not slightly problematical concept is found within black communities and is called "Ubuntu": the philosophy that everyone should help his neighbour by donating time, money and manpower to ensure the survival of even the poorest members of the community. Nowadays this concept is being put into question by the more affluent younger members especially when the idea of support is primarily understood in financial terms and your own wage has to be shared among the entire family.

FOOD & DRINK

Just as the country, there is no single definition of what constitutes South African cuisine. Anything but boring, it is a beguiling fusion of many different cultural influences which provide good reasons why South Africa has become a gourmet mecca.

Each culture, region and ethnic group has its own speciality, usually served in extremely large portions. Cape cuisine has been strongly influenced by Malaysian cooking with their delicious *stews* called *potjies* (pronounced: poikies) while in Natal you should order one of the fiery *seafood curries* with chutney. Inviting guests over for a weekend *braai* (a barbecue) is almost a national sport in South Africa. The meat cooked on the barbecue usually comprises of *boerewors* (traditional sausages) and steaks, which are cooked to suit the particular preferences of the barbecuing class. The white upper class prefer their steaks thickly cut and medium rare while most black families like them thinly cut and well done. Either way, the steaks are delicious and are usually accompanied with creamy spinach, pumpkin and *pap*, a polenta-style maize dish which tastes rather bland but constitutes the staple diet of many South Africans.

Fish is available everywhere, even inland you cannot go wrong by ordering breaded *hake & chips*. Sea food is best enjoyed along the coast and the *line fish* is the seasonal catch of the day. One particular speciality is the *kingklip* with its firm and white meat. Delicacies such

A gourmet feast awaits the visitor with a dizzying array of Asian, Indian, European and local cuisine to tantalise the taste buds

as oysters and lobster – in South Africa the crayfish – cost a fraction of the price you'd pay back home. But what about *vegetarians* we hear you cry? Non-meat eaters should stick to the bigger cities where vegetarian and vegan restaurants are popping up on every corner. Another alternative is to nourish yourself on side dishes: cheap, sun-ripened *fruit and vegetables* are available in abundance and the quality is excellent. Passion fruits and mangos, known as *grenadillas,* are definitely worth trying. You can even *taste the sunshine* in the avocados. Gooseberry jam is the perfect souvenir made from the physalis berry (Cape gooseberry).

You can safely drink tap water wherever you go, but it's always worth asking first if it is suitable for drinking. Bottled *mineral water* only became popular in the late 90s and sparkling water is even more difficult to find. Cold fizzy drinks, on the other hand, are available in every refrigerator and the beer is often served ice-cold. While South Africa's favourite tipple was once brandy with cola, a new

LOCAL SPECIALITIES

Biltong – this popular snack is air dried fillet of beef or game usually sliced very thinly. Every butchers has its own mixture of spices and herbs

Bobotie – a curried lamb mince casserole spiced with apricots, marmalade, raisins and almonds, topped with an egg and milk mixture and then baked. Served with saffron rice and bananas. Sounds peculiar, tastes amazing!

Bredie – meat stew with vegetables, particularly good with tomatoes (photo left)

Bunny Chow – the hit from Durban is a hollowed out loaf of bread filled with curry. Mainly eaten using the fingers

Chakalaka – salad or spicy sauce made from onions, carrots, beans, chilli and tomatoes which is served at braai

Droë Wors – a dry cured sausage, ideal for unrefrigerated storage

Isibindi – thinly sliced lamb liver with onions

Kingklip – a popular South African saltwater fish and a member of the cod family. It has a firm and white meat and is usually served to the table fileted

Koeksisters – very sweet and sticky, a plaited dough delicacy that is deep fried and dunked in syrup before serving

Pap – a maize porridge (similar to polenta) that the Afrikaans community calls pap and eats with *sous* (a tomato and onion sauce) but that actually has its origins in the black African diet where this fairly dry mash plays an important role in the everyday diet. It is called *putu* and is served with *amasi* (a sauce made of sour milk)

Perlemon – also called abalone is a large shellfish found in the Atlantic Ocean, by now greatly endangered by poaching

Potjiekos – a dish of potatoes, meat and vegetables stacked in layers in a cast iron potjie that will stew over an open fire for up to five hours

Samoosa – small, triangular deep fried pastry parcels stuffed with a vegetable or meat filling (photo right)– a greeting from Indian cuisine

Sosaties – kebabs of lamb, dried fruit, tomatoes and onions usually flame grilled

scene is now emerging with *craft beer and craft liquors* such as gin, rum, vodka and whisky. Make sure you try them when you get the chance.

South Africa's wine industry is booming since the end of the apartheid. Although wine has been grown in the country for over 300 years, the real breakthrough only came at the start of the 21st century. The selection of South African wines available in the UK is only a fraction of what you can find in the *wine paradise along the Western Cape*. The wine routes from Constantia, Franschhoek and Stellenbosch, around Hermanus and Robertson Valley are spectacular – however it is a good idea to limit yourself to a maximum of three wine-tastings a day. Recommendations for good vineyards include Constantia Glen, La Motte, Holden Manz, Jordan, Hamilton Russell, Springfield or Tokara.

The quality of coffee varies. On the one hand, the country is witnessing a boom with specialised coffee shops serving *aromatic brews*. However, instant coffee is still served for breakfast in most rural places. Although the taste is not quite as bad as its reputation, the main coffee substitute in South Africa is rooibos tea (see p. 23).

Together with wine, this flavoursome tea has revolutionised the country's *gastronomy*. The choice of restaurants and bistros in cities is overwhelming with new food concepts appearing all the time. And the best news: everything is inexpensive for European wallets. South Africa does not award stars to its restaurants as in Europe – if it did, the country would reach Milky Way status. The tourist is simply forced into trying everything, for better or worse. Expect to put on a few pounds during your stay but you will be rewarded with fabulous memories of the *southern hemisphere's cuisine*. Beware that some restaurants do not have a license to serve

alcohol but charge only a small *corkage fee* if you want to bring your own.

The best time for *lunch* is from noon to 2.30pm, *dinner* is usually served

"Country of origin: South Africa" has long been a seal of quality when it comes to wine

between 6.30pm and 9pm. The daily rhythm takes some getting used to for Northern Europeans: South Africans live by the sun's schedule, joining the rush hour at the fitness studio a at five and leaving pubs promptly at 10pm. It is important to book a table in advance. Many restaurants are closed on Sunday and Monday evenings. The *Eat Out* food bible is the best way to find out about where to eat and drink and is available to buy as a magazine at the airport or online at *www.eatout.co.za*

SHOPPING

Anyone who comes to South Africa with a full suitcase will regret it one week into their holiday at the latest. Souvenirs from South Africa are artistic, exotic and not expensive. Finding exactly the right memento to take home for yourself or a gift for family or friends can be a daunting task: afro print clothing, homemade jewellery, design accessories and traditional arts and crafts will leave you spoilt for choice in the markets and shopping malls. You can spend a whole day browsing through all the stores.

ARTS & CRAFTS

Carved wooden statues are the undisputed classic souvenir. Indeed a man-size giraffe or tapestry is a real eyecatcher in any living room. The rules of thumb when buying goods are always take a good look around before you decide and be sure to haggle the price. A lot of what is on offer is mass produced in factories in neighbouring countries and not as you would expect from a local workshop.

If it is authentic art that you are after (e.g. bronze statues) then it is best to get advice from a specialised dealer. Otherwise have fun bartering the price of goods with local sellers. The Zulu and Xhosa for example, send love letters in the form of small beaded messages that hang from safety pins. The Zulu also make calabash bowls from pumpkins. Embroidered clothes and handbags are typically made by the Xhosa. The Ndebele on the other hand are renowned for their leather loincloths and dolls in traditional garb that embody fertility. In some stores the profits from the sale of traditional arts and crafts go to charitable causes. In Cape Town: *Wola Nani (Unit 3, Block A, Collingwood Place | 9 Drake Street | www.wolanani.co.za)* or in the *Watersheds* of the V & A Waterfront and *Monkeybiz (61 Wale Street | www.monkeybiz. co.za)*; in Knysna: *The Muse Factory (The Old Goal Complex | 17 Queen Street)*; in Durban: *Woza Moya (26 Old Main Road)*; in Johannesburg: *Art Africa (62 Tyrone Av. Parkview)*; in Durban: *Woza Moya (Ufafa Valley | www.wozamoya.org.za)*.

JEWELLERY

The price of gold and diamonds is the same wherever you go. However it is worth checking out the jewellery shops as you pay far less for craftsmanship in South Africa. If in doubt, check if the shop is a certified member of the *Jewellery Council of South Africa.* For those on

Beads, jewellery, leather and much more: Leave space in your suitcase and release your credit card – South Africa is a paradise for souvenirs

a shoestring budget, the jewellers at the *Oriental Plaza* in the Johannesburg district of Fordsburg are hidden gems.

LEATHER

Both jewellery and leather craftsmanship is less expensive here than in Europe which brings down the price of the final product. The Woodstock district in Cape Town is renowned for its selection of small workshops selling handbags, wallets, tablet cases in a variety of colours and in excellent quality (e.g. *www.chapelgoods. co.za | www.dark-horse.co.za | www. rowdybags.com*). Ostrich leather is best bought at speciality stores to avoid buying fakes.

OUTDOOR CLOTHING

Not everything has to be in khaki but sturdy walking shoes are definitely recommended as is long, casual clothing to repel mosquitoes and for bush walks.

There is a wide range of outdoor shops yet neither the quality nor the price of products is better than back home. Your best bet is the *Cape Union Mart* chain *(www.capeunionmart.co.za)*. Most large malls have an outlet.

WINE

South Africa is a veritable paradise for wine connoisseurs. Many of its wine estates offer wine tasting and will ship your purchases home for you – important to bear this in mind as you are only permitted to take two bottles through customs when you leave the country. A premium bottle of wine can set you back 100 rand but even a cheap 25 rand bottle will be decent enough. A good idea is to refer to the John Platter Wine Guide *(www.wine onaplatter.com)* which gives an overview of all the estates and rates their wines. The Pinotage is a red wine grape which is South Africa's signature variety and is a cross between Pinot Noir and Cinsault.

CAPE PROVINCES

The Cape provinces comprise 60 per cent of the country's surface area and offers some rather extreme contrasts. From the dry Kalahari Desert in the north to the dense forests of the Garden Route in the east and in the centre, the semi-desert Karoo. Some may find the isolation of the Karoo intimidating; others will see it as a place of silence and solace.

One of the main attractions is the ★ *Garden Route* along the Indian Ocean – it extends from the small industrial town of Mossel Bay to the mouth of the Storms River. Tourists should not expect to see rows on rows of neatly kept gardens along the Indian Ocean coastline; the name comes from the verdant vegetation and landscape encountered here. The climate is mild all year round. The MARCO POLO Cape Town travel guide will have more in-depth information.

The west coast of the Cape is much drier and more rugged than the *Garden Route*. The resort town of *Langebaan* with its lagoon is reminiscent of the Mediterranean while the interior here opens up into desert-like *Namaqualand* which transforms into a sea of wild flowers between August and October after the rains. The *Vanrhyns Pass* in the Northern Cape is the best vantage point from which to view this spectacular sight.

Even further in the north lies the fascinating Kalahari Desert with the *Kgalagadi Transfrontier National Park,* a wildlife reserve barely touched by tourism. Stretching across a huge section of South Africa and Namibia, there are no border

Photo: Railway bridge near Knysna

Desert and lush greenery: be it barren wilderness or idyllic forests – outdoor fans will be in seventh heaven

fences and the game can move freely, as can tourists. The dramatic *Augrabies* waterfalls are at their awe-inspiring best when the Gariep River *(Orange River)* floods and huge volumes of water plunge some 56m (183ft) into the ravine. Port Elizabeth, today part of the Nelson Mandela Bay municipality, is the capital of the Eastern Cape. The province is home to the Xhosa tribe to which Nelson Mandela belonged. A few kilometres on is the *Addo Elephant Park*, home to elephants and as well as a number of other wild animals.

GEORGE

(135 E5–6) *(Ø F8)* **The capital of the Garden Route (pop. 200,000) lies at the foot of the Outeniqua Mountains and is surrounded by an idyllic park-like landscape.**

Travelling from the Karoo, you reach George via the Montagu or Outeniqua Pass. It's worth to take a stroll around the town. Don't be deceived though: some sources would have you believe that the

Old Slave Tree marks the spot where slaves were once tied up to be traded. This isn't true: the old chain hanging from the tree was used to fasten up equipment from the neighbouring tennis court. Also seum including the first ever engine to be driven in Johannesburg. A unique experience awaits you when you travel on the *Power Van* which powers its way up the  pass where you can enjoy a picnic

Curious fledgling: the area around Oudtshoorn is the centre for ostrich breeding

worth a visit is *St Mark's Cathedral*, Africa's smallest cathedral.

with panoramic views at the top. *2 Mission Street | Mon–Sat 8am–5pm | admission 40 rand*

SIGHTSEEING

GARDEN ROUTE BOTANICAL GARDEN ●

These attractive gardens are popular for picnics; amateur botanists and disc golf enthusiasts can also have fun exploring what the park has to offer. *49 Caledon Street | daily 7am–6pm | admission 10 rand*

OUTENIQUA TRANSPORT MUSEUM

This museum is a playground for young and old and will bring a tear to the eyes of any avid railway enthusiast. 13 old steam engines are on display in the mu-

FOOD & DRINK

LAUREN'S

This tiny deli is a hit with anyone looking for light, tasty and filling snacks and meals from good coffee and oriental dishes to creamy curries. Everyone will leave full and happy. *44 Eden Meander Lifestyle Centre | Knysna Road | tel. 07 98 97 23 25 | Budget*

OLD TOWNHOUSE

Traditional dishes are the hallmark of this restaurant located in one of the city's oldest buildings. *Corner York Street/*

Market Street| tel. 04 48 74 36 63 | Moderate

LEISURE & SPORTS

The *Outeniqua Farmers Market (Sat 8am–2pm)* across from the Garden Route Mall is the place to go on Saturday mornings for breakfast and a stroll around the stalls – and then it's off on your surfboard to the tiny Victoria Bay for the afternoon. The INSIDER TIP Silverspray B & B *(3 rooms | tel. 08 25 12 18 48 | www.silverspray.co.za | Budget)* lies just 6 m (20 ft) from the sea.

WHERE TO STAY

FANCOURT ★

This delightful country estate dating back to 1860 has one of South Africa's best golf resorts but also features a spa and several pools for non-golfers looking to lie back and relax. Fancourt has been praised for its water conservation measures in the maintenance of its golf courses. *115 rooms, 18 suites, 10 self-catering houses | Montagu Street| tel. 04 48 04 00 00 | www.fancourt.com | Expensive*

GARDENVILLA

It's hard to decide what to like most about this romantic B&B: the idyllic Cape-Dutch style manor house or the breakfast buffet with the best quality organic ingredients. *5 rooms | 35 Plantation Road | tel. 04 48 74 03 91 | www.gardenvilla.co.za | Moderate*

INFORMATION

GEORGE TOURISM OFFICE

124 York Street | tel. 04 48 01 92 95 | www.georgetourism.org.za

WHERE TO GO

CANGO CAVES ★ (135 E5) *(F8)*

These underground caves some 80km (50mi) north-west of George are among the world's most fascinating stalagmite and stalactite caves. The gigantic limestone hollows and claustrophobic tunnels are still under exploration. *Guided tours* or *adventure tours (60 or 90 minutes) on the hour or half hour from 9am to 4pm | admission 100–150 rand*

MARCO POLO HIGHLIGHTS

★ Garden Route
South Africa's famous coastal route along the Indian Ocean making your loved ones at home green with envy → p. 32

★ Fancourt
You want to be a golf ball so you could spend all year on the grounds of this luxury hotel → p. 35

★ Cango Caves
The artworks in these stalagmite and stalactite caves have formed in 20 million years → p. 35

★ Kgalagadi Transfrontier Park
It is only here that you can observe wild animals with dual citizenships → p. 41

★ West Coast National Park
Bring the book of bird species! The wetland conservation area is home to many birds and blooming plants → p. 45

★ Addo Elephant National Park
Mini elephants in action soooo cute! → p. 48

Endless amount of space at the beguiling beach in Wilderness

OUDTSHOORN (135 E5) (*⊞ F8*)

Oudtshoorn is the centre of the ostrich farming community. Located 70 km (43 miles) from George it is the world's most successful ostrich farming area. Ostriches have been farmed in Oudtshoorn since 1860 when ostrich feathers became highly fashionable accessories among European nobility. The value of the feathers equalled almost that of gold and turned ostrich farmers into extremely rich barons. Find out what caused the decline of this once lucrative industry at the *C. P. Nel Museum (3 Baron von Rheede Street | Mon–Fri 8am–5pm, Sat 9am–1pm | admission 25 rand)* or take a tour of one of the farms, e.g. the ● *Cango Ostrich Farm (admission 100 rand | tel. 04 42 72 46 23 | www.cangoostrich.co.za)* to learn more about today's ostrich farming methods. Out of town, on the road to the Cango Caves, is the original B & B *Le Petit Karoo Ranch (10 rooms | tel. 04 42 72 74 28 | www.lepetitkaroo.co.za | Moderate)* with jacuzzi behind the safari tent.

WILDERNESS (135 E5) (*⊞ F8*)

The town of Wilderness is located at the mouth of the Kaaiman River. Its 5km (3mi) long beach makes this a popular holiday choice. The best hotel in the area is INSIDER TIP *Views Boutique Hotel & Spa (26 rooms | South Street | tel. 04 48 77 80 00 www.viewshotel.co.za | Expensive)* which is set high up above the beach and has spectacular ocean views. *Eden Adventures (tel. 04 48 77 01 79 | www.eden.co.za)* organises canoe rides on the Wilderness lagoon and through the national park which the N2 coastal road cuts through.

GRAAFF-REINET

(135 F4) (*⊞ G7*) **This hidden gem appears out of nowhere in the middle of the Karoo semidesert. Graaff-Reinet**

(pop. 40,000) is one of South Africa's oldest towns and is surrounded by the *Camdeboo National Park.*

The city centre feels like a large outdoor museum with architecture spanning the past 200 years. From simple Karoo huts through to stately Cape Dutch homes (replicas of homes built in Amsterdam in the 18th century) to Victorian cottages, all beautifully restored.

SIGHTSEEING

REINET HOUSE MUSEUM

furniture and household utensils, as well as bicycles. The grapevine in front of the building was planted in 1870 and is thought to be the oldest in the country. *Murray Street | Mon–Fri 8am–4pm, Sat/Sun 9am–1pm | admission 20 rand*

FOOD & DRINK

DE CAMDEBOO

Located on the grounds of the noble *Drostdy Hotel,* this is the perfect venue for those looking to celebrate a special occasion and with a large appetite for meat; the portions are enormous. A whisky at the bar will help after the meal. *Church Street 30 | tel. 04 98 92 21 61 | Moderate*

POLKA

The place to relax during the day and celebrate at night. Its delightful courtyard is the perfect setting to enjoy the restaurant's ciabatta pizza and the region's specialty, slow-cooked Karoo lamb. *52 Somerset Street | tel. 08 75 50 13 63 | Budget*

SHOPPING

WINDMILL JUNCTION

From antiquities and art to bric-a-brac and kitsch, owner Amori offers every-thing in traditional Karoo design in her tiny browsing shop. *52 Somerset Street*

WHERE TO STAY

KAMBRO COTTAGE

Although it is located in the middle of town, this small B & B will offer you a quiet and relaxed stay. *2 rooms | 73 Somerset Street | tel. 04 98 91 03 60 | kambrocottage@gmail.com | Budget*

SOMERSET STABLES

In 1997 Reinette Te Water Naude bought a large garden with stables which now accommodates visitors who would prefer to stay forever. *3 rooms | 39 Donkin Street | tel. 08 36 68 62 10 | Budget*

INFORMATION

TOURISM BUREAU

13a Church Street | tel. 04 98 92 42 48 | www.graaffreinet.co.za

WHERE TO GO

CAMDEBOO NATIONAL PARK
(135 F4) (*Ø G7*)

The national park's main attraction is the ⬩*Valley of Desolation (daily from sunrise to sunset | admission 80 rand),* a series of dramatic and sheer cliff faces that stand sentry over an isolated valley. Stay over at the *Mount Camdeboo Private Game Reserve (11 rooms | tel. 04 98 91 05 70 | www.mountcamdeboo.com | Expensive | 60 km/37 miles from Graaff-Reinet*

CRADOCK (136 A5) (*Ø H7*)

Cradock is a small very typical Karoo town. South African author Olive Schreiner wrote her 1883 classic, "The Story of an African Farm" here and the *Olive Schreiner House (9 Cross Street)* commemorates her life. 25 Victorian houses in Market Street have been extensively refurbished to form part of the small hotel INSIDERTIP Tuishuise (36 Market Street | tel. 04 88 81 13 22 | www.tuishuise.co.za | Moderate). 100 km/62 miles from Graaff-Reinet

MOUNTAIN ZEBRA NATIONAL PARK (136 A4) (*∅ H7*)

This national park was established in 1937 to prevent the extinction of the Cape Mountain Zebra. Lions and cheetahs are their companions. (Information tel. 04 88 81 24 27 | admission 167 rand | www.sanparks.org/parks/mountain_zebra). 170 km/105 miles from Graaff-Reinet

GRAHAMS-TOWN

(136 B5) (*∅ H7*) **Home to students, ghosts, churches and a festival - what else does a town need to attract visitors?**

When the British founded this town in 1812 (today's pop. 70,000), they didn't reckon with the resistance of the local Xhosa tribes. They launched a ferocious and bloody attack against the colonial forces which perhaps explains the large number of churches in the town – to pacify the Gods. The population of this small university town doubles in size every July, transforming itself into a venue for the National Arts Festival (www.nationalartsfestival.co.za) for an entire week.

SIGHTSEEING

OBSERVATORY MUSEUM

The watchmaker Henry Carter Galpin used to invite guests into his house, promising them unique views from the topmost tower. They were indeed treated to a live panorama of the town from above through a system of lenses and mirror, known as a camera obscura, which is the only one of its kind in the country today. The building is slightly outdates but still interesting to visit. Bathurst Street | Mon–Fri 9am–4.30pm, Sat 9.30am–1pm | admission 10 rand

FOOD & DRINK

HARICOT'S DELI & BISTRO

Pastries and breads to die for in this deli, which transforms into a French-Mediterranean bistro in the evenings. 32 New Street | tel. 04 66 22 21 50 | Budget

WHERE TO STAY

8A GRAHAMSTOWN ☆

Cushions, cushions everywhere in this delightful hotel offering splendid views over the town. A luxury guesthouse with affordable room prices. 5 rooms | 8A St Aidans Av. | tel. 07 21 59 48 05 | www.8agrahamstown.co.za | Moderate

INFORMATION

GRAHAMSTOWN TOURISM OFFICE

High Street | tel. 04 66 22 32 41 | www.grahamstown.co.za

WHERE TO GO

HOGSBACK (136 B5) (*∅ J7*)

Could be the name of a place in Middle Earth in "Lord of the Rings"? Maybe, seeing that JRR Tolkien was born in South Africa and Hogsback is often claimed as the author's inspiration for the forest of Mirkwood. This hiking area in the Amathole mountains celebrates its reputation and there are magical attractions in every corner such as the labyrinth of the ☆ The

Edge Mountain Retreat (25 rooms | tel. 04 59 62 11 59 | www.theedge-hogsback. co.za | Budget–Moderate), looking on the Middle Earth landscape from above. And you can sleep and eat well there, too. *140 km/87 miles from Grahamstown*

KWANDWE PRIVATE GAME RESERVE
(128 B5) *(Ω J8)*

This private Big Five park is the perfect retreat for a stress-free holiday. Four lux-

and set in motion the biggest diamond rush of all times.

This discovery laid the foundations of the diamond city *Kimberley* (pop. 230,000). Eureka – the first diamond to be found – was 21.75 carats. A replica is on display in the mine museum. Initially the prospectors only searched the river banks but as more and more arrived from around the world, the search expanded away from the river into the

Views into the Big Hole from the viewing platform in Kimberley

ury lodges provide everything you need to relax *(see also Kwandwe Ecca Lodge, Sp 115)*. *22 rooms | Heatherton Towers | Fort Brown | tel. 04 66 03 34 00 | Expensive | 20 km/12.5 miles from Grahamstown*

KIMBERLEY

(136 A2) *(Ω G–H5)* **In 1866 the teenager Erasmus found a glistening stone while loitering down at the Gariep River**

earth itself. At first Kimberley was little more than a tent city known by the diggers as *New Rush.* By 1870 some 50,000 people were digging for diamonds in the so-called *Big Hole*, the world's largest man-made excavation. It is 215 m (705 ft) deep, has a diameter of 1.6 km (1 mile) and covers an area of 42 acres. 43 years of mining yielded 2722 kg (6000 lb) of diamonds equivalent to 13.6 million carats. The tent city developed into a small city which was named Kimberley in 1873.

KIMBERLEY

SIGHTSEEING

BIG HOLE AND KIMBERLEY MINE MUSEUM ● ⛷

The viewing platform spans the crater of the Big Hole – if you passed the „head for heights" test, you can take a picture as a reward. The old part of the city is an open air museum of historical houses. The *Visitors' Centre* depicts the history of the diamond rush and uncut diamonds are displayed in the *Diamond Vault*, among them the famous '616', a 616 carat diamond crystal. *Tucker Street | daily 8am–5pm | the museum is admission free, the Big Hole admission fee is 100 rand*

MCGREGOR MUSEUM

Don't be overwhelmed by the abundance of information on display in this museum. Originally built as a sanatorium, the exhibitions cover diverse topics, from the history of civilisation to the wealth of the diamond magnates. *Atlas Street | Mon–Sat 9am–5pm, Sun 2–5pm | admission 25 rand*

FOOD & DRINK

OCCIDENTAL BAR & RESTAURANT

A liquor and a plate full of authentic South African food served on the long western-style bar are the perfect way to end the day. *Tucker Street/Big Hole Complex | tel. 05 38 32 26 68 | Budget*

WHERE TO STAY

CECIL JOHN RHODES GUEST HOUSE

Guests here are transported back in time to the diamond rush era but the amenities are all very modern. *8 rooms | 138 Du Toitspan Road | tel. 05 38 30 25 00 | www.ceciljohnrhodes.co.za | Budget*

PROTEA HOTEL KIMBERLEY

Don't lean out too far over the edge. Cocktails served on the patio give you an awesome view deep into the crater. *94 rooms | West Circular Road | tel. 05 38 02 82 00 | www.proteahotels.com | Moderate*

INFORMATION

TOURIST INFORMATION CENTRE

121 Bultfontein Road | tel. 05 38 30 67 79 | www.kimberley.co.za

WHERE TO GO

AUGRABIES FALLS (134 C1) (*Ø E5*)

The original Khoi residents named the waterfall *Aukoerebis* – "place of big noises". A fitting description, especially when you are standing in front of these im-

The waters of the Orange River make their way through the rock: Augrabies Falls

pressive waterfalls cascading almost 60 m/200 ft down from a lunar landscape into the depths below. Rumour has it that there are diamonds at the bottom of the pool. Any attempts at diving for them would however be futile due to the force of the water *(7am–6pm | admission 176 rand)*. The *Dundi Lodge* 3 km (1.8 mile) from the falls is your best bet for an overnight stay in this area *(11 rooms | tel. 05 44 51 92 00 | www.dundi lodge.co.za | Moderate)*. Some 500km *(310 miles) west of Kimberley*

KGALAGADI TRANSFRONTIER NATIONAL PARK ★
(130–131 C–D 2–4) (*⌗ E–F 2–3)***

Straddling the border between South Africa and Botswana, this park is the world's largest untouched ecosystem. You can get up close and personal to many of its four-legged inhabitants, especially if you spend the night in one of the park's unfenced wild camps. Often booked out well in advance. *Daily 7.30am–sunset | admission 304 rand | www.sanparks.org/parks/kgalagadi. 600 km (373 miles) northwest of Kimberley*

TSWALU KALAHARI GAME RESERVE ⬤
(131 E4) (*⌗ G4)***

An oasis in the middle of the desert established by the Oppenheimer diamond family not just to create a private retreat for the family but to restore the Kalahari to itself with exemplary ecotourism. Highlight for the night: INSIDER TIP a bed under starry skies. *14 rooms in lodges | near Kuruman | tel. 05 37 81 93 31 | www.tswalu.com | Expensive. 380 km (236 miles) from Kimberley*

KNYSNA

(135 E6) (🕮 G8) **Knysna (pop. 35,000) is a charming, colourful town and the unofficial capital of the Garden Route.** The town lies between a mountain range and a large lagoon that is connected to the sea by a narrow stretch of water. At the lagoon mouth are two sandstone cliffs, the *Knysna Heads,* one on each side of the lagoon. Start by walking around the town and follow it up with a sundowner – a truly unique experience. Another attraction is the Knysna Forest, a rainforest embedded in the surrounding mountains. This small town is a popular holiday resort for South Africans who were naturally devastated by the forest fires which broke out in June 2017 when a storm hit the area. Thousands of people lost their houses or huts; it will take some time to repair the devastation wrought by the fires.

FOOD & DRINK

ILE DE PAIN BREAD & CAFÉ

Exquisite fresh bread and pastries and beautiful architecture leave you no choice but to stay for breakfast or lunch. *10 Boatshed | Thesen Island | tel. 04 43 02 57 07 | Budget*

INSIDER TIP TOTTIE'S FARM KITCHEN

A nondescript timber shack from the outside, the interior is quaintly decorated with Grandma's lace doilies and flower-painted teacups to create a comfortable, vintage and creative interior. The owners Garth and Marian van Reenen refuse to serve fast food, preferring freshly made, generous portions of country food served at lovingly decorated wooden tables. Buffet on Sundays. *Main Road | Rheenendal | tel. 04 43 89 00 92 | Budget*

ZACHARY'S

High up above the lagoon in the Conrad Pezula Hotel is the best restaurant on the Garden Route, all dishes are made with organic produce. *Conrad Pezula Hotel | tel. 04 43 02 33 33 | Expensive*

SHOPPING

KNYSNA FINE ART

One of the country's best galleries showcasing some of the best, if not priceless, paintings. *6 Long Street*

THE WATERFRONT

All kinds of quaint shops can be found around the yacht harbour, among these is the *Beach House* where you can buy the perfect sailing outfit. *Knysna Quays*

LEISURE & SPORTS

The three *Elephant Hiking Trails* are between 6 and 9 km (3 to 5 miles) in length through spectacular, verdant vegetation. The best way to go elephant-watching is with a guide. For golfers there is the *Pezula Golf Club (tel. 04 43 02 53 33)* in its spectacular setting. Water sport options are endless and if you are after something out of the ordinary then rent a houseboat for your overnight stay: *Knysna House Boats (tel. 04 43 82 28 02 | www.knysna-houseboats.com | Moderate)*. You can hire a boat from *Knysna Charters (Quay Four | Thesens Island | tel. 08 28 92 04 69)*.

ENTERTAINMENT

THE PROJECT BAR

Choosing the right sundowner in this bar can be a difficult decision to make. Then sit back, relax and take a selfie in front of the skyline. Located slightly hidden on the 1st floor of the Sirocco Building. *Thesen Island | www.theprojectbar.co.za*

Easy going pace with splendid views: waterfront restaurant at Knysna harbour

WHERE TO STAY

HOMTINI GUEST FARM ● ☀

The glamping equivalent of a farm holiday. Guests are accommodated in spacious cottages with their own veranda or in luxury permanent tents with splendid views over the green Outeniqua mountains. The farm has its own pool. It is the starting point for several great hiking trails. *8 rooms| Homtini Pass | tel. 07 27 27 87 17 | www.homtini. co.za | Moderate*

INSIDER TIP TURBINE HOTEL ☺

The architecture and interior design of this former power station are electrifying: relax at the original wood boiler and dine under the labyrinth of pipelines overhead. The establishment also meets eco-friendly standards. Including spa, restaurant and café. *24 rooms | 36 Sawtooth Lane | Thesens Harbour Town | tel.*

04 43 02 57 46 | www.turbinehotel.co.za | Expensive

WATERFRONT LODGE ☀

The name says it all. It's left up to the guests to decide whether they want to bathe in the lagoon or their own extra-large bathtub. *8 rooms | On the Point | tel. 04 43 82 16 96 | www.waterfront-lodge.co.za | Moderate*

INFORMATION

KNYSNA TOURISM

40 Main Street | tel. 04 43 82 55 10 | www. visitknysna.co.za

WHERE TO GO

PLETTENBERG BAY (135 E6) (*Ω G8*)

Once you have mastered the pronunciation of *Knysna,* the next thing to learn is that most South Africans don't know this town's full name, calling it simply "Plett". Even fewer are probably aware of the fact that this beautiful bay was in fact originally called: *Bahia Formosa*. Today Plettenberg Bay is an exclusive holiday resort with three beautiful beaches which are great for families. On average the sun shines 320 days a year here and

two adventurers. The view over the Bitou River makes it the perfect romantic setting *(8 rooms | Bitou Valley | tel. 04 45 01 25 00 | www.emilymoon.co.za | Expensive)*.

Above the famous Lookout Beach is the small *La Vista* guest house with its captivating views of the sea ☆ from the pool deck *(7 rooms | 17 Rosheen Cres-*

Suspension bridge straddling the Storm River in the Tsitsikamma National Park

between July and September whales give birth to their young in the bay.

Right on the rocks at the water's edge is the luxury hotel ☆ *The Plettenberg* with unrivalled sea views. Its restaurant *Seafood* is the best in town *(37 rooms | Look Out Rocks | tel. 04 45 33 20 30 | www.collectionmcgrath.com/plett | Expensive)*.

A few kilometres outside of town is INSIDER TIP ▶ *Emily Moon River Lodge*. This hotel is an ode to the love between

cent | tel. 04 45 33 54 07 | www.lavista. co.za | Moderate). Recommended restaurants include the *Fat Fish (Hopwood Street | tel. 04 45 33 47 40 | Moderate)* and the eco-conscious 🌊 *Le Fournil de Plett (Lookout Centre | tel. 04 45 33 13 90 | Budget)*. 🌊 *Ocean Blue Adventures (tel. 04 45 33 50 83)* offers dolphin and whale viewing by boat trips. The company follows the strict guidelines set out by nature conservation.

10 km (6 miles) outside of town you will come across South Africa's most beautiful tree house hotel, the ☀️ *Tsala Treetop Lodge* – surrounded by ancient milkwood trees *(16 rooms | tel. 04 45 01 11 11 | www.tsala.hunterhotels. com | Expensive)*.

TSITSIKAMMA NATIONAL PARK
(135 F6) *(🗺 G8)*

This nature reserve not only encompasses indigenous rainforests and dramatic coastlines, it also stretches 5km/3mi out to sea. Day visitors (admission 196 rand) are invited to walk over the ☀️ suspension bridge which spans the mouth of the Storm River or explore the forest and its inhabitants on a multi-day hike. The best place to listen to the concert of crickets and frogs at night in the park is from the *At The Woods* guesthouse *(4 rooms | Storms River | tel. 08 23 28 23 71 | www. atthewoods.co.za | Moderte)*. Adventure seekers may want stop in at outdoor activity operator *Stormsriver Adventure (tel. 04 22 81 18 36 | www.storms river.com).* who offer an action-packed programme of events including canopy walks and a woodcutters tour.

LANGEBAAN

(134 B5) *(🗺 D7)* **This small sleepy town (pop. 8500) lies right on the Langebaan lagoon and is a true bird lover's paradise.**

In the summer it is home to some 55,000 birds including herons, ibis, oystercatchers, greater and lesser flamingos and cormorants. Langebaan is a good base for exploring the *West Coast National Park* (main entrance to the south of the resort) but windsurfers, kayakers, fishermen and divers also appreciate Langebaan mainly because of the warm water. It is a fantastic place to learn kitesurfing.

SIGHTSEEING

WEST COAST NATIONAL PARK ⭐

Situated on the west coast to the north of Cape Town, this small national park is home to the Slow Five: tortoises, sand tiger sharks, porcupines and the Cape dune mole-rats endemic to the Cape who are great to watch burrowing into the ground. The park is famous for its wildflower display, which is usually between August and October. A road runs around

STEP INTO THE UNKNOWN

There is no money-back guarantee at *Face Adrenalin (www.faceadrenalin. com)*. Those who decide to bungee-jump have to go through with it. It can be a daunting experience, especially when you see the pale faces of the other jumpers waiting in the middle of the Bloukrans Bridge (N2 coastal road). The highest bungee jump in the world involves throwing yourself 216 m/700 ft into the

unknown. But if Prince Harry can do it, it can't be too difficult! The friendly staff will give you a final push over the edge to send you speeding down the canyon towards the Bloukrans River below before the cord pulls you out of your free-fall into a huge pendulum swing. Spectators are also charged for watching their friends: it costs 150 rand to accompany a jumper up to the bridge.

the lagoon and there are hiking trails as well as boat and bird-watching tours.

FOOD & DRINK

INSIDER TIP STRANDLOPER

Hordes of prawns line up on the beach over an open fire – just one of ten courses to be served at this beach restaurant. Make sure you book in advance and plan to spend a whole day here so take along a few games. Does not accept credit cards! *Tel. 02 27 72 24 90 | www. strandloper.com | Budget*

WHERE TO STAY

CHRYSTAL LAGOON LODGE

Gaze out of the lodge's wide, spacious windows and cherish the extraordinary beauty of the nature around. Located on a dune of Calypso Beach, a wooden walkway leads you from the lodge down to the beach below. *10 rooms | 52 Casos Road/at the Calypso Beach Estate | tel. 02 27 72 05 50 | www. westcoastlife.co.za | Moderate*

INFORMATION

LANGEBAAN TOURISM BUREAU

Bree Street/Hoof Street | tel. 02 27 72 15 15 | www.langebaan-info.co.za

WHERE TO GO

PATERNOSTER (134 B5) (Ⅲ D7)

Many a shipwrecked sailor has probably said his final prayers off the shores of this romantic fishing village. You can also offer prayers of thanks when you enter the delightful *ah! Guest House (5 rooms | 1 Mosselbank Street | tel. 08 24 64 58 98 | www. ahguesthouse.com | Moderate)*. Treat yourself to some of the best west coast seafood at the *Noisy Oyster (tel. 02 27 52 21 96 | Budget)*. 40 km (25 miles) from Langebaan

PORT ELIZABETH

(136 A6) (Ⅲ H8) This harbour city (pop. 350,000) was named after the wife of its founder, Sir Rufane Donkin. South Africans simply call it 'PE'.

Everything started with an English fort built in 1799. Today PE is the centre of the country's motor vehicle industry: Ford, Opel and Volkswagen are all manufactured here. Except for the city's Victorian heritage, many tourists fail to appreciate the city's charm at first glance. Port Elizabeth's main attractions lie outside the city centre and on the long sandy beaches.

SIGHTSEEING

CAMPANILE ⚘

A touch of Venice in Africa. Built in 1923, this 53 m (173 ft) tower is a memorial to commemorate the first landing of the British in Port Elizabeth and offers – after ascending 200 steps – an excellent view of the city. Its bells chime at 8.22am, 1.32pm and 6.02pm. *Strand Street | Tue–Sat 9am–12.30pm and 1.30–5pm*

CITY WHERE TO START?
Market Square is the historical part of PE with some noteworthy buildings like the city hall. From here head west to Donkin Street with its Victorian houses. Housed in the Donkin Lighthouse Building, the tourist information centre is the starting point for the art walking trails through the park. Leave your car on one of the attended car parks.

NO. 7 CASTLE HILL MUSEUM

Museum complex with a settler's house dating from 1827, the city's oldest building which was originally built as the rectory. *7 Castle Hill Street | Mon–Thu 9am–*

1951. The museum traces the company's history using informative and interactive platforms. Golf carts whizz you through the factory next door. *Daily 8.30am–4pm | admission 10 rand | 103 Algoa Road | Uitenhag*

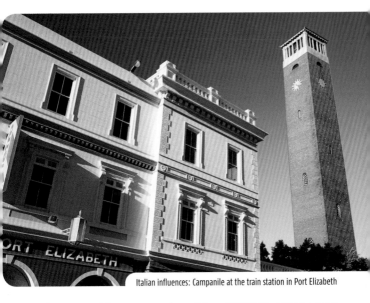

Italian influences: Campanile at the train station in Port Elizabeth

1pm and 2–4.30pm, Fri 10am–1pm and 2pm–4pm | admission 10 rand

ST GEORGES PARK

Besides sports fields, playgrounds, an open-air theatre and swimming pool, the well-maintained "Central Park of PE" is also home to the *Nelson Mandela Metropolitan Art Museum* which showcases works from Eastern Cape artists and the *Botanical Gardens* full of different species of plants.

VOLKSWAGEN AUTO PAVILION

A VW car museum is an attraction in a country where many still drive around in City Golfs. The first sedan (later known as the "Beetle") left the production line in

FOOD & DRINK

FRIENDLY STRANGER

What's the rule again...Don't talk to strangers? You are invited to eat with them though in this creative boathouse far away from the sea. Hearty food is served on enamel plates at a good value for money. *1 Bridge Street | tel. 07 49 11 97 08 | Budget*

GINGER THE RESTAURANT ⬩⬩

Boasting a nice view, Ginger is a cool restaurant situated right on the beachfront (in *The Beach Hotel*) in Summerstrand. The deliciously tasting fish starters are particularly recommended. *1 Marine Drive | tel. 04 15 83 12 29 | Moderate*

INSIDER TIP THIS IS EAT

A jewel in the port's crown. Quaint wooden benches, red sun parasols and fish on the daily menu. Sushi replaces curry in this restaurant and the chef is known for having his off days. A fact which apparently doesn't deter the queue of guests in front of the restaurant. *On the harbour | tel. 04 15 28 21 61 | Budget*

SHOPPING

OLD CURIOSITY SHOP

This curiosity shop is a paradise for collectors of Victorian silver and porcelain. *8 Lawrence Street*

LEISURE & SPORTS

Surfing gear can be hired on just about every beach and you can also scuba dive in the ship wrecks off the coast *(Pro Dive | tel. 04 15 811 144)*. And *Sundays River Adventures (tel. 07 11 85 65 65 | www.sun-daysriveradventures.com)* can show you how to go sandboarding on the beach.

ENTERTAINMENT

BRIDGE STREET BREWERY

The home-brewed beer and tapas are excellent. Live music is often performed on Friday and Saturday evenings. *1 Bridge Street*

CUBANA

Very modern, Latino bar lounge with views of the ocean and port. *Beach Road | McArthur Centre | tel. 04 15 85 52 82*

WHERE TO STAY

LAVENDER TERRACE B&B

Most tourists only spend one night in PE – owner Ginny is keen to make it an enjoyable experience for her guests. *2 rooms, 1 cottage | 25 Marshall Road | Humewood | tel. 04 15 82 22 00 | Budget*

NO 5 BOUTIQUE ART HOTEL

Appealing to lovers of art and literature, this hotel is reminiscent of The Great Gatsby: start with a drink from the Art Deco minibar followed by a plunge in the spa to take your worries away. *10 rooms | 5 Brighton Drive | tel. 04 15 02 60 00 | www.no5boutiquearthotel.com | Expensive*

INFORMATION

NELSON MANDELA BAY TOURISM

Donkin Lighthouse Building | tel. 04 15 82 25 75 | www.nmbt.co.za

WHERE TO GO

ADDO ELEPHANT NATIONAL PARK ★
(136 A5–6) (*Ø H7–8*)

More than 600 elephants in more than 415,000 acres of national park, 60 km

LOW BUDGET

One of South Africa's most popular hiking trails is the *Otter Trail* on the Garden Route. It takes five days and you need to book it a year in advance. If you are travelling alone or as a couple, it's always worth inquiring if any spaces have become available. Without booking or payment, you can still walk the first day of the hike that begins at the mouth of the Storms River.

A stop at the Billabong and Quiksilver *factory shops* in Jeffrey's Bay is an absolute must for dirt cheap surfing gear.

A welcome refreshment at the watering hole: elephant in the Addo Elephant National Park

(37 miles) from Port Elizabeth. When the reserve was opened in 1931 it had only eleven elephants. Today it is also home to the Big Five (buffalo, elephant, lion, leopard and rhino) and the park has expanded into the sea and now also includes southern right whales and great white sharks i.e the Big Seven. *7am–7pm daily | admission 250 rand*

As in almost all the state-run parks, accommodation is available within the Addo grounds. Located next to a large watering hole, the *Main Camp (42 rooms | tel. 01 24 28 91 11 | www.sanparks.org/parks/addo | Moderate)* is particularly recommended for its views of the animals drinking even after a game drive. Remember to book well in advance. If you haven't reserved a room and you're looking for a spot of luxury, check out the *Gorah Elephant Camp (11 rooms | tel. 04 45 01 11 11 | www.gorah. hunterhotels.com | Expensive)*. This privately owned camp is situated in the mid-

dle of the park. 5 km (3 miles) from the main entrance is the *Addo Dung Beetle Guest Farm (12 rooms | tel. 08 39 74 58 02 | www.addodungbeetle.co.za | Moderate)*.

JEFFREY'S BAY ● (136 A6) (*ω H8*)

Usually shortened to "J-Bay", this small coastal resort offers the best waves for surfing throughout South Africa. What was once a laid-back hippy commune has transformed into a mecca for surfers from all over the world. Both guesthouses from *African Perfection (14 rooms | 20 Pepper Street | tel. 04 22 93 14 01 | www.africa nperfection.co.za | Moderate)* are situated directly on Supertube beach. Make sure you book a INSIDER TIP corner room on the first floor for a sea view. Don your best surfing outfit and employ the services of a surfing instructor at *Surf-Jbay (tel. 04 22 96 03 76 | www.surf-jbay.co.za)* to teach you the basics. *80 km (50 miles) from Port Elizabeth*

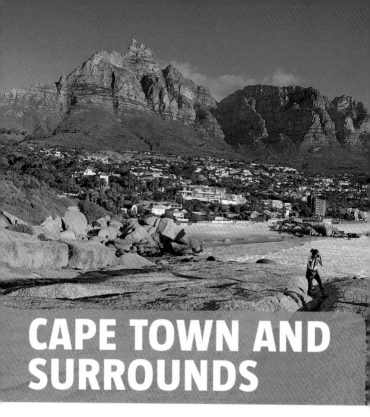

CAPE TOWN AND SURROUNDS

To set things straight from the start: Cape Town is not South Africa. The city is more like the European dream of Africa which has been evolving constantly since the 17th century. Its beauty is undeniable – some of the sunsets over the city are so memorizing that you are left shaking your head in amazement.

The city's colonial heritage is visible on every corner, in the city centre planning and on the faces of its inhabitants – in no other South African city will you see more white people. Capetonians share the same mentality as others who live by the sea around the world: they are slightly crazy, mad about sports and take a laissez-faire approach to life. Cape Town is South Africa's pin-up girl: tourists are captivated by the city's beauty, taking hundreds of photos to impress friends back home. Anyone who sees the photos will immediately start looking for flights, and those who have already been and can afford it are sure to return.

You should schedule at least five days in your travel agenda to visit Cape Town. The time spent in this beguiling city will fly by. And the surrounding region is just as enticing with the legendary Cape of Good Hope being a must on your to do list. So are the spectacular Winelands destinations of Constantia, Franschhoek, Stellenbosch and Paarl where the French Huguenots once settled and brought their magnificent vines with them. Or the bustling town of Hermanus, which is the second home of the southern right and humpback whales during South Africa's winter.

Hardly a more beautiful spot on the planet: Cape Town is bold, vibrant, pushy, down-to-earth and above all laissez-faire

CITY WHERE TO START?

The ideal starting point to set out from on a first stroll through the city is **Greenmarket Square**. From here head past the old city hall to St George's Cathedral. Behind the church is where the beautiful green Company Gardens begin. You will find parking spaces in the side streets around or in Loop Street or Long Street.

CAPE TOWN

MAP INSIDE THE BACK COVER
(134 B5–6) (𝑚 D8) Both seasoned travellers and locals are of the opinion that Cape Town (pop. 3.7 million) is the world's most beautiful city.
You get the best view of Cape Town when you arrive by ship. The sight of the city extending up the slopes of the mountain is awe-inspiring as is Table Mountain itself, draped by a "tablecloth" of clouds on

Imaginative murals: boy in the Bo-Kaap district

most mornings from November to April. In the bay beneath the mountain lies the harbour. The rocky seabed meant that it had to be built far out to sea in order to attain the depths needed. The oldest section surrounding the Victoria and Alfred basins have now been converted in to the popular *Victoria & Alfred Waterfront* entertainment area with restaurants, shops, museums and theatres.

Cape Town's economy is based on its tourism and its commercial harbour. Spoilt by their magnificent surroundings Capetonians are cheerful, easy going and know how to make the most of their city. Their laissez faire approach to life means that they seldom get worked up or stressed out, an attitude jokingly known as the "Cape coma".

At the tip of the peninsula is the Cape of Good Hope and this is where the Atlantic and Indian Oceans meet. The water along the coast warms up as you travel further east, one of the reasons why Hermanus is such a popular destination. The town is also renowned as the world's best land-based whale watching loca-

tion. Between June and December the females give birth in the bay. Further up the coast, near to Bredasdrop is Africa's most southerly tip, Cape Agulhas. Less spectacular than the Cape of Good Hope yet spectacularly rugged and authentic. The MARCO POLO Cape Town travel guide will have more in-depth information.

SIGHTSEEING

BO-KAAP (MALAY QUARTER) ★
(U B3) (*ω b3*)

A vividly painted district, full of history – the neighbourhood's tiny houses were built by freed slaves and their descendants still live here. Stroll through the district and up its steep lanes, taking in its exotic smells and listening to the muezzin calls resounding from the mosque. Always ask before taking a photo.

CASTLE OF GOOD HOPE ●
(U C5–6) (*ω c5–6*)

Fortified with canons this fortress, South Africa's oldest building, was built in 1666 as the residence of the first governor of the

Cape and to protect the settlers. The ghosts of dead prisoners have apparently been spotted floating through the castle walls. *Corner Darling Street/Buitenkant Street | Mon–Sat 9am–4pm | guided tours Mon–Sat 11am, noon and 2pm | admission 30 rand*

DISTRICT SIX MUSEUM (U B5) (𝄢 b5)

Apartheid is when suddenly someone comes and says "You can't live here anymore, everything will be demolished tomorrow". This exhibition covers life before and after the forced evictions and guided tours are organised with eye witnesses. *25 Buitenkant Street | Mon–Sat 9am–4pm | admission 45 rand*

GROOT CONSTANTIA ● (0) (𝄢 0)

This is the oldest wine estate in Africa and the manor house is a particularly impressive example of Cape Dutch architecture. Wine tastings are possible, and at the restaurant *Jonkershuis (tel. 02 17 94 62 55 | Moderate)* you can enjoy Cape cuisine in a historical courtyard. *Groot Constantia Road | 9am–6pm*

KIRSTENBOSCH BOTANICAL GARDENS ★ (0) (𝄢 0)

On the eastern slopes of Table Mountain at a height of 100m (328ft) to 1000m (3280ft) are the famed botanical gardens. The park offers a tree canopy walkway, summer concerts, restaurants and thousands of suitable picnic spots. August to October is the best time to admire the remarkable displays of spring blossoms. *Daily Sept–March 8am–7pm, April–Aug 8am–6pm | admission 50 rand*

INSIDER TIP ▶ LION'S HEAD (0) (𝄢 0)

Every Capetonian has to have climbed up the Lion's Head at least once in his lifetime. Peaking at 700 m/2195 ft above sea level, the climb starts gradually, increasing in steepness towards the top. It's a local ritual to hike up and watch the sun go down on a full-moon night. Don't forget to take a headlamp, pullover, snacks and maybe even a bottle of wine with you. Consult the route online beforehand!

⭐ **Kirstenbosch Botanical Gardens**
The best time to visit is during the South African spring which is from August to October → p. 53

⭐ **Table Mountain**
The fit and adventurous can hike up to the 1000 m (328 0ft) summit but there is always the cable car option → p. 54

⭐ **Bo-Kaap**
The city's most colourful district in stark contrast to its gentrified surroundings. And it's proud of its distinctness → p. 52

⭐ **Cape of Good Hope**
Windswept and monumental sight. Where once seafarers crashed their ships, tourists now stand in queues to take the perfect souvenir photo → p.58

⭐ **Spiceroute**
A chocolatier, a guardian of family recipes and a grappa king: culinary delights on a hill near Paarl → p. 62

⭐ **Stellenbosch**
A delightful and historic town (one of South Africa's oldest) right in the middle of the wine producing area → p. 63

MARCO POLO HIGHLIGHTS

ROBBEN ISLAND MUSEUM (0) (*0*)

It is somehow perfidious to ban freedom fighters to an island in the hope that they are simply forgotten about. Of his total of 27 years in prison, Nelson Mandela spent 18 years incarcerated on Robben Island. Former prisoners still take visitors on a tour through the cells. If you plan to visit the island, you should reserve a seat on the ferry in advance (daily 9am, 11am, 1pm and 3pm). The tour lasts around three hours and is a slightly commercial attraction yet a definite must-see. *Clocktower Terminal | Waterfront | admission 320 rand | tel. 02 14 13 42 00 | www.robben-island.org.za*

TABLE MOUNTAIN ★ ⊰⊱ (0) (*0*)

No visit to Cape Town is complete without the mandatory trip up Table Mountain. It takes the cable car only five minutes to reach the summit 1086m (3562ft) above the city. There are also a number of hiking paths like the ● *Platteklip Gorge* route, which starts at the cable car station in the valley. You have a panoramic view over the entire Cape peninsula from the summit. The cable car runs all year round weather permitting (price approx. 255 rand). The *Sundowner Special* after 6pm in summer is INSIDER TIP half price and is the perfect opportunity to watch the sun set over the Atlantic. *Table Mountain Road | cable car schedule: www.tablemountain.net | weather information tel. 02 14 24 81 81*

VICTORIA & ALFRED WATERFRONT ●
(U E–F1–2) (*e–f1–2*)

There are many reasons to keep coming back to the V & A Waterfront: for a helicopter flight or boat tour around the Cape, to fill up on sea food or just to see and be seen. The oldest part of the harbour has been under extension for years as well as the entertainment precinct with its hotels, museums, restaurants and shopping boulevards. The complex was named after Queen Victoria and her son Alfred who laid its foundation stone in 1860. It is referred to as the V & A Waterfront by the South Africans; another display of their foible for abbreviations. On a rainy day, head to the underwater world at *Two Oceans Aquarium (9.30am–6pm daily | admission 150 rand | www.aquarium.co.za) | V & A Waterfront Information Centre (Mon–Sun 9am–6pm | tel. 02 14 08 76 00 | www.waterfront.co.za)*

FOOD & DRINK

Where to start, where to end and where to go in between? The choice is overwhelming, the advice and tips on *www.eatout.co.za* and *www.tripadvisor.com* may or may not help you decide.

GRAND CAFÉ & BEACH ● (0) (*0*)

Cape Town's only restaurant on the beach is in Granger Bay next to the Waterfront and is the perfect spot to enjoy your sundowners with your feet in the sand. *Granger Bay | tel. 02 14 25 05 51 | Expensive*

CAPE TOWN AND SURROUNDS

MARCO'S AFRICAN PLACE
(U C3) (*c3*)

Africa on your plate. Chef Marco Radebe was the first black gastronomer in Cape Town – since 1997 he invites guests to Bo-Kaap to taste lots of different African dishes. *15 Rose Street | Bo-Kaap | tel. 02 14 23 54 12 | Budget*

INSIDERTIP PANAMA JACK'S
(O) (*0*)

Ship ahoy! Drink like a sailor and eat like a fisherman in this fisherman's retreat which serves fresh fish straight to the table. This wooden shack lies in the midst of the container port – the friendly men at the entrance barrier will help you if you can't find it. *Quay 500 | harbour | tel. 02 14 48 10 80 | Moderate*

THE TEST KITCHEN (O) (*0*)

Agreed to be the best restaurant in Africa, this establishment is not just about good eating, it offers a complete sensory experience over 15 courses. Reservations are taken on the first day of the month for the next calendar month. The *Pot Luck Club* (see p. 19) is close by and offers deluxe tapas and a rooftop glasshouse. *375 Al-*

bert Road | Woodstock | tel. 02 14 47 23 37 | www.thetestkitchen.co.za | Expensive

VERGELEGEN ᠅ (O) (*0*)

Despite being over 300 years old, this wine estate looks anything but dated. There are two top-class restaurants and the delicious picnic with all trimmings served in the middle of the forest is a big hit with visitors. Reservation is essential. *Lourensford Road | Somerset West | tel. 02 18 47 21 00 | Moderate*

SHOPPING

INSIDERTIP BREE STREET
(U B–C3) (*b–c3*)

Hipster alert! When you stroll down this street that is constantly reinventing itself, you should watch your credit card. There are many temptations in the form of fashion, jewellery, ceramics, bags – all of it original and often handmade. Take a deep breath and have a bite to eat, for example at the *Jason Bakery* or at *La Parada*.

UWE KOETTER (U C2–3) (*c2–3*)

Said to be the best jeweller in Cape Town. The creations in his shop in De Waterkant

Shopping and entertainment centre: Victoria & Alfred Waterfront

55

make ladies' eyes sparkle. Cape Town is, after all, popular for proposals... *Cape Quarter Lifestyle Village | 27 Somerset Road*

ly 9am–9pm | Dock Road | V&A Waterfront | www.waterfront.co.za/shop/watershed

MONKEY BIZ ⊕ (U B3) (𝄞 b3)

A craft project that offers employment opportunities to disadvantaged women. Their beadwork animals certainly cannot be found on every street corner. *61 Wale Street | Bo Kaap | www.monkeybiz.co.za*

THE WATERSHED (U F1) (𝄞 f1)

The nicest place to shop for hours for the perfect souvenirs. Housed in a former warehouse, there of rows and rows of stalls selling designer items. Snacks are available next door in the food court. *Dai-*

FOR FILM BUFFS

Mandela: Long Walk to Freedom is an impressive film directed by Justin Chadwick based on the life of Nelson Mandela (2013) which chronicles his struggle for freedom and justice in emotional scenes with the fantastic Idris Elba starring in the lead role. The film was the most expensive South African film production of all time – Mandela died the month in which the film was released.

Tsotsi means „gangster" in township slang: the Tsotsis are either honoured or feared. The film tells the story of David set in the slums of Johannesburg where murder is an everyday occurrence and your future is decided for you before you even start school. This is until a baby is suddenly discovered in the back seat *of* a stolen car.... The film with Kwaito soundtrack won an Oscar in 2006.

LEISURE & SPORTS

Cape Town lives on, around, in and from the water. The V&A Waterfront is lined with numerous boat tour operators like *Mirage (tel. 07 12 66 05 01)*. Or do you prefer to be the captain of your own ship? Then contact *Ocean Image (tel. 06 37 87 81 45)*. For a round of morning golf, go to the *Steenberg Golf Estate (tel. 02 17 15 02 27)* followed by the spa in the ● *One & Only Hotel (tel. 02 14 31 58 88)*, to pamper yourself with a baobab oil massage. The nicest beaches are the bays around Clifton.

ENTERTAINMENT

In the evening most of the action takes place at the *V&A Waterfront (U F1–2) (𝄞 f1–2)* or in the centre around *Long Street* and *Kloof Street (U A4) (𝄞 a4)*. Also worth a mention:

ORPHANAGE COCKTAIL EMPORIUM (U A3) (𝄞 a3)

Behind the old city walls, this bar attracts a cool and beautiful clientele: the cocktails mixed by the tattooed barmen are worth every penny. *227 Bree Street*

PLANET BAR ⩐ (0) (𝄞 0)

The bar belonging to the *Mount Nelson* colonial hotel is THE place to dress up. Sip your drinks slowly in style as they are extremely expensive. *76 Orange Street*

WHERE TO STAY

INSIDER TIP ▸ THE BACKPACK ⊕ ⩐ (0) (𝄞 0)

Couch surfing with a Ritz-style service. The rooms are decorated in brightly col-

Waiting for buyers: the delightful beaded creations from Monkey Biz

oured, relaxing colours and the view of the Tafelberg from the pool would usually cost double. Super location and committed to sustainable tourism. *15 rooms | 74 New Church Street | tel. 02 14 23 45 30 | www.backpackers.co.za | Moderate*

GRAND DADDY (U C4) (ⓜ c4)
Chic hotel with a super bar and excellent restaurant is in the middle of the city. If you stay here you can spend the night in an American *Airstream Trailer* on the roof. *26 rooms | 38 Long Street | tel. 02 14 24 72 47 | www.granddaddy.co.za | Expensive*

KOPANONG B & B (0) (ⓜ 0)
A tiny township guest house in Khayelitsha. The proprietor Thope is a typical African mama and likes to escort her guests around the hood. *3 rooms | C 329 Velani Crescent | tel. 02 13 61 20 84 | www.kopanong-township.co.za | Budget*

PROTEA HOTEL FIRE AND ICE
(U B3) (ⓜ b3)
Cool hotel with macabre touches such as the shark cage lift and cof-
fins in the smoker's room. *105 rooms | New Church/corner Victoria Street | tel. 02 14 88 25 55 | www.protea.mariott. com | Expensive*

STEENBERG COUNTRY HOTEL ●
(0) (ⓜ 0)
Guests at this country hotel don't have to drive the 30 km/18 miles into Cape Town: everything they require can be found on the grounds of the exclusive Steenberg estate, namely wine, golf and spa. To top it all: two excellent restaurants, *Catharina's* and *Bistro 1682*. *35 rooms | Tokai Road | Constantia | tel. 02 17 13 22 22 | www.steenbergfarm. com | Expensive*

INFORMATION

CAPE TOWN TOURISM (U C4) (ⓜ c4)
Castle/corner of Burg Street | tel. 02 14 87 68 00 | tourismcapetown.co.za

V&A WATERFRONT INFORMATION CENTRE (U E2) (ⓜ e2)
Dock Road | tel. 02 14 08 76 00

CHAPMAN'S PEAK DRIVE ⅍
(134 B6) (*ℳ D8*)

The route from *Hout Bay* to the Cape of Good Hope is via this spectacular coastal drive. In the 1920s the road was hewn from the mountain rock face. The 9 km (5.6 mile) drive cuts through overhanging rocky outcrops and its 114 bends wind high above the lashing ocean. It is well worth every cent of the 42 rand toll fee per car. *15 km (9.3 miles) from Cape Town*

CAPE OF GOOD HOPE ★ ⅍
(134 B6) (*ℳ D8*)

The Cape of Good Hope is at the southernmost tip of the peninsula and forms part of a nature reserve. The Atlantic and Indian Oceans do not flow into each other here: the official dividing line is at Cape Agulhas. When Bartholomew Diaz first sailed around the Cape he called it the Cape of Storms. True to its name the weather can be volatile here. Once there, a funicular takes you up 40 m (131 ft) to the top of *Cape Point* then you have 133 steps to climb to reach the lighthouse. The vantage point gives you a breathtaking view of the sea and the peninsula. *Oct–Mar 6am–6pm daily, April–Sept 7am–5pm | admission 165 rand and 65 rand for the funicular | 65 km (40 miles) from Cape Town*

SIMON'S TOWN (134 B6) (*ℳ D8*)

Since 1814, *Simon's Town* (40 km/25 miles from Cape Town) has been a naval base – and a great destination on the return from the Cape. The coastal stretch a few kilometres further south is of particular interest for its penguin colony. There is a viewing platform where you can watch their antics or you can swim with them at the neighbouring beach *(Boulders Beach | admission 70 rand)*. After a stroll through Simon's Town you can eat right

there at *Saveur (Wharf Street/Boardwalk Centre | tel. 02 17 86 19 19 | Moderate)* or at the seafood temple *Harbour House (tel. 02 17 88 41 33 | Expensive)* in Kalk Bay.

FRANSCH-HOEK

(134 B–C5) (*ℳ D8*) **Eat, drink and sleep is the motto of Franschhoek. Or was it sleep, eat and drink?**

The small town (pop. 16,000) of Franschhoek invites visitors to daydream about opening their own winery. The number of cafés, shops and restaurants has tripled in the last few years. You will always find the perfect spot to enjoy the sunset with a bottle of chilled Sauvignon Blanc. Franschhoek was founded by the French Huguenots in 1688 who had fled persecution in their homeland. Luckily they brought their vines with them. The fertile valleys surrounded by picture-postcard mountains became perfect to exercise their viticulture skills. Even today many of the wine estates have French names. The selection of vineyards is staggering as is the choice of delicious cuisine to accompany the wine.

INSIDER TIP ▶ FRANSCHHOEK MOTOR MUSEUM ●

To stop yourself drinking too much wine, visit this fun museum which has a collection of over 200 vintage cars. By the way, the museum is on the *L'Ormarins* farm – yet another round of wine-tasting. *Mon–Fri 10am–6pm, Sat/Sun 10am–5pm | admission 80 rand*

FRANSCHHOEK PASS ● ⅍

It is worth taking a drive up the most beautiful mountain pass just as you leave Franschhoek. The first settlers called it Elephant Pass because herds of elephants used it as a route into the valley. Today you get a fantastic view of the vineyards and orchards.

FOOD & DRINK

THE KITCHEN AT MAISON
The chef resembles a rock star or surfer, his dishes use a maximum of four ingredients plucked fresh from the farm. The restaurant boasts a stylish yet laid-back ambience and you've struck gold if you've got a seat on the veranda. *Maison Wine Estate | tel. 02 18 76 21 16 | Moderate*

INSIDER TIP LA PETITE FERME ☼
Neither small nor secluded, this ostentatious wine estate serves rather conservative food yet it is the best place to watch the sun setting. There is no nicer view over the Franschhoek valley except maybe from the mountain pass above, which should however be avoided if you've been tasting wine. *Franschhoek Pass Road | tel. 02 18 76 30 16 | Moderate*

SHOPPING

THE CERAMICS GALLERY
Fragile beauties: the distinguished ceramicist David Walters invites you to watch him. His house is also home to his gallery and potter's studio. *24 Dirkie Uys Street*

TSONGA ✪
Finally a reputable place selling 100% made in Africa shoes and handbags, handmade by Zulu women. *40 Huguenot Street*

WHERE TO STAY

AUBERGE CLERMONT
A feeling of Provence under the African sun. Surrounded by vineyards the estate's old

Ready to march: penguins on Boulders Beach

wine cellar has been converted into guest rooms. *6 rooms | Robertsvlei Road | tel. 02 18 76 37 00 | www.clermont.co.za | Expensive*

INSIDER TIP LA RESIDENCE ☼
This ultra-luxury accommodation would have been fit for any French King. Each room is furnished in a unique colour and style. Not to forget the breathtaking mountain scenery around. *16 rooms | Elandskloof Private Road | tel. 02 18 76 41 00 | www.laresidence.co.za | Expensive*

INFORMATION

FRANSCHHOEK WINE VALLEY AND TOURISM ASSOCIATION
62 Huguenot Road | tel. 02 18 76 28 61 | www.franschhoek.org.za

Perfect backdrop for a new Facebook profile photo: the wild coastline near Hermanus

WHERE TO GO

BABYLONSTOREN 🌿
(134 B5) *(⚏ D–E8)*

One of the region's oldest and most verdant wine farms. The paradise gardens are divided into 15 sections in order to let nature take its course. The staff brings baskets full of the fruit and vegetables harvested to the restaurant *Babel (tel. 02 18 63 38 52 | Expensive)* and to the bistro *Greenhouse daily 10am–4pm | Budget)* every morning. They also have wines, of course *(tasting Mon–Sun 10am–5pm). 28 km/17 miles from Franschhoek*

HERMANUS

(134 C6) *(⚏ D8)* **Hermanus (pop. 33,000) is surrounded by mountains and the scents of the sea. The farmers who settled here back in the 19th century would surely never have believed that you could earn a living as a whale crier.** Since 1992, Hermanus has had the world's only whale crier who sounds his kelp horn to announce a sighting of whales as between July and December, large numbers of ● southern right whales make their appearance in Walker Bay. Although this small town has been commercialised by tourism, it is still a good base to explore the region's long sandy beaches and the wine area of Hemel en Aarde which are still there once the whales have departed.

SIGHTSEEING

CLIFF PATH

Pack a picnic and off you go – it is roughly 12 km/7 miles between the New Harbour in the west and the pretty Grotto Beach in the east. The best way to return is by steam train.

FOOD & DRINK

BIENTANGS CAVE ⚉

A remarkable cliff-side setting definitely worth a stop for the fish and seafood specialities. Watch out though: the spray from the whales below can reach you on the harbour. *Below Marine Drive | tel. 02 83 12 34 54 | Moderate*

INSIDER**TIP** THE CUCKOO TREE

One of the restaurants which locals prefer to keep a secret. A small and laid-back establishment with a tiny garden and a clear focus on the essentials: home-cooked food served by warm-hearted staff. *155 Dirkie Uys Street | tel. 02 83 12 34 30 | Budget*

JUST PURE BISTRO 🐾

Coffee served with a sea breeze and breakfast with sea views through the bistro's high windows in case it gets too windy outside. *Marine Drive/Park Lane | tel. 02 83 13 11 93 | Budget*

LEISURE & SPORTS

Thrilling adventure: shark diving is an amazing experience. 🐾 *Marine Dynamics Shark Tours (Kleinbaai | tel. 07 99 30 96 94 | www.sharkwatchsa.com)* guarantees a marine biologist on every trip to ensure the protection of both man and animal. If you're looking to get up close and personal to the whales, contact its sister company, the ecotour operator *Dyer Island Cruises (tel. 08 28 01 80 14 | www.whalewatchsa.com)*.

WHERE TO STAY

BIRKENHEAD HOUSE 🐾

This hotel is in the best location high up on the cliffs above the bay with amazing views out to sea and access to a lovely beach. *11 rooms | 119 11th Street | tel. 02 83 14 80 00 | www.birkenheadhouse.com | Expensive*

WINDSOR HOTEL 🐾

The same fantastic view but for a snip of the price. The location is magnificent even if the hotel has a slightly outdated charm. *60 rooms | 49 Marine Drive | tel. 02 83 12 37 27 | www.windsorhotel.co.za | Moderate*

INFORMATION

HERMANUS TOURISM BUREAU

Old Station Building | Mitchell Street/corner Lord Roberts Street | tel. 02 83 12 26 29 | www.hermanustourism.info

WHERE TO GO

STANFORD (134 C6) (*Ø E8*)

Sleepy, laid-back artist villages where everyone knows each other can be found everywhere. 20 minutes after leaving Hermanus, slow down and enjoy the new pace of life in Stanford. Enjoy an ice cream at the exiled Italian *Don Gelato* followed by lunch at *Marianas (12 Du Toit Street | tel. 02 83 41 02 72 | Budget)*. And if you become thirsty, try the wine estate Springfontein with INSIDER**TIP** restaurant run by the acclaimed German chef Jürgen Schneider, who has discovered the free-

LOW BUDGET

Dinner on the beach: in Hout Bay you can buy fresh fish at the harbour in the morning and have a braai on the beach in the evening accompanied by a good wine. Don't forget to take the obligatory photo of the sunset.

For quirky design at backpacker prices opt for *Daddy Long Legs* on trendy Long Street. *13 rooms | 134 Long Street | tel. 02 14 22 30 74 | www.daddylonglegs.co.za*

dom of cooking between the ☆ vineyards and mountains. *Tel. 02 83 41 06 51 | www.springfontein.co.za | Expensive*

PAARL

(134 B5) (⑩ D8) Paarl (pop. 112,000) is the largest town in the wine lands. Its name derives from the massive granite rock above the town that shimmers like a pearl when the sun catches it.

It was here in 1875 that the world's youngest language – Afrikaans – was declared an official language. A monument that pays tribute to this. It was from Paarl's *Victor Verster,* now called *Groot Drakenstein Prison*, that Nelson Mandela was released in 1990.

SIGHTSEEING

AFRIKAANS LANGUAGE MONUMENT
It resembles the gateway to an outer galactic civilisation and is supposed to symbolise the influences of different languages and cultures on Afrikaans itself. It's worth a photo stop. *April–Nov 8am–5pm, Dec–March 8am–8pm | admission 25 rand | Gabbema Doordrift Street*

SPICEROUTE ★ ☆
Probably the most popular trail among gourmets. The farm is home to a fine selection of local producers, specialising in chocolate making, beer brewing and other decorative accessories. The panorama also invites you to gaze out over the mountains beyond. *www.spiceroute.co.za*

FOOD & DRINK

BLACKSMITH'S KITCHEN ☆
Where a blacksmith once heated up his iron, the chef now takes his potatoes from the fire oven to serve to guests in a delightful courtyard in front of the magnificent backdrop of Paarl. *Pearl Mountain Weingut | Bo Lang Street | tel. 02 18 72 95 07 | Expensive*

FOR BOOKWORMS

Born a Crime – Trevor Noah is South African's comedy superstar: the shows of this deadpan comedian focus on comical everyday life situations which have his audiences screaming in laughter, regardless of their nationality or skin colour. But Noah's life has not always been filled with laughter. He was born in Johannesburg, the son of a white Swiss father and a Xhosa lady during apartheid, when it was illegal for mixed-race couples to procreate. The stories Noah tells of his childhood are amazing, absurd, sad and still drop dead funny (2017). Watch some of his shows on video before reading.

We are no such things (2016) – a compelling account seeking an alternative narrative for the case of Amy Biehl by author Justine van der Leun. The 26-year old US American, Amy Biehl, was killed by a township mob in 1993. Was she simply in the wrong place at the wrong time? Two of the convicted men now work in the foundation set up in Amy's honour and have become substitute children for Amy's parents. The book attempts to clarify how this could happen and what really happened that afternoon – a fascinating lesson in history.

The symbolisation is not obvious at first glance: Afrikaans Language Monument in Paarl

NOOP

The chef couple Zian and Mariette keep their menu simple in their historic house. A venue for special occasions. *127 Main Street | tel. 02 18 63 39 52 | Expensive*

WHERE TO STAY

INSIDER TIP 5 KONINGS ACCOMODATION

Regal rooms at affordable prices. The owner Rachelle offers access to families and has just extended her guesthouse due to its popularity. *8 rooms | 5 Koning Street | tel. 08 44 00 45 25 | Expensive*

INFORMATION

PAARL TOURISM BUREAU
216 Main Road | tel. 02 18 72 48 42 | www. paarlonline.com

WHERE TO GO

WELLINGTON (138 B5) (*D8*)
This small sleepy town (pop. 55,000) was founded in 1840 and is characterised by its Victorian architecture. Today the *Welling-ton Wine Route* is growing in popularity. On the historical wine estate INSIDER TIP *Doolhof* the manor house has been converted into the *Grand Dédale* country hotel *(7 rooms | Rustenburg Road | tel. 02 18 73 40 89 | www.granddedale.com | Expensive)*. A paradise for wine lovers and sports enthusiasts with a vast range of activities from horse riding to rafting. *20 km (12.5 miles) from Paarl*

WILDERER DISTILLERY
(134 B5) (*D8*)
Between Paarl and Franschhoek, Helmut Wilderer distils the best liquors of the cape on a small farm *(daily 10am–5pm)*. The restaurant serves light lunches *(on the R 45 | tel. 02 18 63 35 55 | Budget)*. *7 km (4.3 miles) from Paarl*

STELLEN-BOSCH

(138 B5) (*D8*) ★ **Stellenbosch (pop. 155,000) and its surrounds is South Africa's most import wine producing region,**

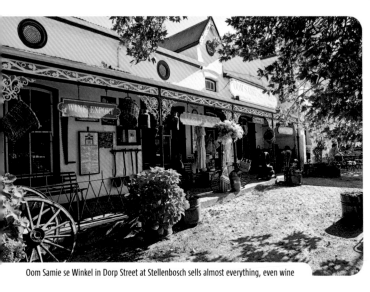

Oom Samie se Winkel in Dorp Street at Stellenbosch sells almost everything, even wine

and the historic old town centre is particularly charming.

South Africa's second oldest town's name goes back to Cape governor Simon van der Stel, who started a settlement here in 1679. A stroll through the town's oak lined streets will take you straight back in time – that is, until a crowd of students starts to make noiose in one of the cafés, for Stellenbosch is a popular university town. The historical centre with its well-preserved Cape Dutch and Victorian buildings has a special atmosphere.

SIGHTSEEING

DORP STREET ●

Artistic gables are the trademark of this street's listed Cape Dutch houses. The 1851 Lutheran church today houses the university art gallery. *Oom Samie se Winkel* is a village store that is run today as it was yesteryear. Selling traditional sweets and old-fashioned food items, bric-a-brac and even antiquities. Light meals served in the garden *(84 Dorp Street | tel. 02 18 87 07 97 | Budget)*.

VILLAGE MUSEUM

Until when did the Victorian era last? Why are the roof gables on Dorp Street so decorative? Find out for yourself on this group of four exquisitely restored and period-furnished houses in this museum. The houses help to bring history to life. *18 Ryneveld Street | Mon–Sat 9am–5pm, Sun 9–3pm | admission 30 rand*

FOOD & DRINK

BIG EASY

This restaurant is partly owned by the famous golfer Ernie Els (known as the Big Easy); you cannot miss his trophies and photos on display inside. The dress code is casual-sporty (polo shirts are a must) and the high quality of food will impress the most notorious of golf joke tellers. *95 Dorp Street | tel. 02 18 87 34 62 | Moderate*

INSIDER TIP RESTAURANT AT CLOS MALVERNE ☺ 〜

This restaurant doesn't even have its own name – a modest touch for an establishment with its reputation and first-class cuisine. Cape classics are reinterpreted and prepared with produce from their own gardens. Boasts amazing views over the vineyards. *Devon Valley Road | tel. 02 18 65 20 22 | Expensive*

WIJNHUIS

Appealing street bistro and wine bar which attracts a friendly and cheerful crowd. *Church Street/corner Andringa Street | tel. 02 18 87 58 44 | Budget*

SHOPPING

BOEZAART BAUERMEISTER

Delicate lace-inspired fine jewellery by two female designers. *Corner Ryneveld Street/Church Street*

SMAC ART GALLERY

Sells cutting-edge South African art that moves and shakes you. One of the country's best contemporary art galleries. *De Wet Centre | Church Street*

ENTERTAINMENT

BALBOA BALCONY BAR

Good after work vibes on the balcony. Popular with students who prefer more sophisticated venues. The freshly squeezed juices in the cocktails might help to keep guests on an even keel. *18 Andringa Street*

WHERE TO STAY

INSIDER TIP 10 ALEXANDER

Cheap accommodation is impossible to find in Stellenbosch yet this old town-house feels as if you are sleeping over at a friend's parents' place whose style you have always admired. *8 rooms | 10 Alexander Street | tel. 02 18 87 44 14 | www.10alexander.co.za | Expensive*

TWICE CENTRAL

Three friends were inspired to dream up a holiday property that was ultra-modern, luxurious and in the city centre. The result is the Twice Central Guesthouse. *7 rooms | 7 Hamman Street | tel. 02 18 87 78 89 | www.twicecentral.co.za | Expensive*

INFORMATION

STELLENBOSCH TOURISM BUREAU

36 Market Street | tel. 02 18 83 35 84 | www.stellenbosch.travel

WHERE TO GO

STELLENBOSCH WINE ROUTES ●
(134 B5–6) (𝄞 D8)

Before you consider reducing your alcohol consumption, there are over 100 wineries around Stellenbosch waiting to be tested. The first question you are left to decide is in which order to visit them? Help is at hand at *Stellenbosch Wine Routes (36 Market Street | tel. 02 18 86 43 10 | www.wineroute.co.za)*. And the second question is WHO will be driving? *Social Trekking (tel. 06 09 93 59 86 | www.socialtrekking.co.za)* takes every wine taster on an individual and exclusive tour while **INSIDER TIP** *Vine Hopper (Tel. 02 18 82 81 12 | www.adventureshop.co.za)* quite simply offers a hop-on/hop-off wine-tasting tour service.

FREE STATE

The Free State is Boer country. The Afrikaans farmers own the majority of land, cultivating maize, crops and corn. They have also recently diversified to game.
A road trip along the high plateau, on which the province lies, can send a passenger to sleep – the landscape rarely changes, the fields and meadows flash by like on a production line and the roads continue straight on for miles. Nelson Mandela described the province in his autobiography: „The Free State landscape gladdens my heart, no matter what my mood. When I am here I feel that nothing can shut me in and that my thoughts can roam as far as the horizons."
The horizon in the Free State is the borders to six other South African provinces and the Kingdom of Lesotho. It is the only independent state in the world that lies entirely above 1000 m/3281ft in elevation. Lesotho is easily accessible from the small border town of Ladybrand.
In terms of landscape, the Free State becomes more interesting around its perimeter; one particularly impressive sight is encountered on the journey from Harrismith in the northeast to Zastron in the south: mountain range peaks are lined along the right of the road like chickens on a roost. The province takes on a lunar-like landscape around Parys with the Vredefort crater, one of the largest known impact craters in the world. Now measuring around 50 km/30 miles in diameter, the original crater was estimated to have a diameter of roughly 300 km/190 miles. Sci-

**Boring landscape at first glance?
Look closer and this high inland plateau will
reveal a few surprises**

entists have calculated that the asteroid that hit Vredefort would have been approximately 10 km/6.2 miles in diameter. Those Boers, who migrated eastwards from the frontiers and became known as the *Voortrekker,* were obviously oblivious to this occurrence millions of years ago. These Dutch pioneers first had to cross the Orange River – which is why the province was also called the Orange Free State up until the end of the apartheid.

An absolute highlight for trekkers today lies at the foothills of the Maluti Moun-tains: the *Golden Gate Highlands National Park* with its high plateau, golden sandstone outcrops and its diverse wildlife. Once you have crossed the national park and climbed up into the mountains, you will reach the difficult to read and impossible to pronounce settlement of Phutha-ditjhaba, the former capital of the apartheid homeland Qwaqwa. With its lofty mountain peaks and gently undulating meadows at a height of more than 2000 m/6561 ft it is an area straight out of a story book. Home to the Basotho people, it is a landscape made for hiking. This ethnic group is famed for its handicrafts and their exquisitely handwoven woollen rugs and blankets, perfect souvenirs for cold winter evenings back home.

Another option is to soak up the tranquillity of farming life in the Free State by taking the Riemland route from Sasolburg to Rosendal. The name Riemland goes back to when the Boers slaughtered the large herds of wildebeest that

BLOEMFON-TEIN

(136 B2) (ⓂH5) Bloemfontein (pop. 260,000) is the capital of the Free State, a lively university town and seat of the Supreme Court of Appeal – the highest appeal court in South Africa.

Symbol of hope: Mandela statue on Naval Hill in Bloemfontein

roamed here. Their hides were cut into narrow strips called *riempies.* Today antelopes such as South Africa's national animal, the springbok, are left to breed without disturbance on the wild farms in the region. In the middle of the province is the Free State's richest asset, its goldfields, that is considered to be the world's richest producing gold area. A third of South Africa's gold is mined here.

"The city of roses" is what Bloemfontein is popularly known because of the abundance of its gardens and parks. The fact that it is 1400 m (4593 ft) above sea level means that both its summers and winters are mild. Its history goes back to 1840 when Voortrekker Johannes Nicholas Brits settled here. He named his farm after what he could see around him: a water spring surrounded by flowers.

WHERE TO START?
Head to **Herzog Square** in the centre of the city surrounded by the city hall, the National Museum and the Fourth Raadsaal. The Supreme Court of Appeal is on President Brand Street, which also leads to the First Raadsaal. Your best bet for parking is on President Brand Street.

SIGHTSEEING

ANGLO-BOER WAR MUSEUM
The relevance of the years of conflict between the Boers and the British is explained in detail in this exciting museum. It provides a vivid account of this dramatic period with its international ramifications, probably as good, if not better, than any history teacher. *Monument Road | Mon–Fri 8am–4.30pm, Sat 10am–5pm, Sun 11am–5pm | admission 10 rand*

NAVAL HILL
Today you'll spot giraffes standing here rather than naval guns. The Franklin Game Reserve on top of the hill is a wild park in the heart of the city. There are fantastic views of the surrounding landscape and of the skies above in the renovated planetarium. Take a closer look at the gigantic statue of Nelson Mandela on the southern slope to find out what is in his ear. *Daily 8am–5pm | admission free*

FOOD & DRINK

SEVEN ON KELLNER
Creative, colourful, comfortable and with an attention to detail: that goes for both the cuisine and interior design. Mediterranean dishes with a hint of North Africa. Book a table in advance. *7 Kellner Street | tel. 05 14 47 79 28 | Moderate*

STEREO CAFÉ
Even the middle of South Africa is not immune to hipsters. This cool coffee shop has its own roaster and frothy milk with an artistic twist. *60 2nd Av. | tel. 05 14 30 11 35 | Budget*

WHERE TO STAY

HOBBIT BOUTIQUE HOTEL
This small hotel has been named after the city's most famous son: author John Ronald Reuel Tolkien and his hobbit characters from *Lord of the Rings*. Not to be missed: the four-course evening set menu. *12 rooms | 19 President Steyn Ave | tel. 05 14 47 06 63 | www.hobbit.co.za | Moderate*

INSIDER TIP LIEDJIESBOS B&B
An architect with a penchant for design and a secret yearning for the countryside dreamt up this house. 3 km/1.9 mile outside of Bloemfontein, rows of aloes greet the guests. Inside: highly individual furniture, and the guests are spoiled rotten. *5 rooms | 13 Frans Kleynhans Road | Groenvlei | tel. 08 32 82 57 01 | Expensive*

INFORMATION

BLOEMFONTEIN TOURISM
60 Park Road | tel. 05 14 05 84 89 | www.bloemfonteintourism.co.za

⭐ **Golden Gate Highlands National Park**
Impressive sandstone cliffs
→ p.70

⭐ **Lesotho**
Independent mountain kingdom in the middle of South Africa → p. 71

MARCO POLO HIGHLIGHTS

WHERE TO GO

BASOTHO CULTURAL VILLAGE ●
(136 C2) (*Ø K5*)

The *Golden Gate Highlands National Park* gives an insight into how the Basotho have lived for centuries: round huts, animal skins, spiritual healers. You can spend the night in the village, but it's not a must. *Mon–Fri 8am–5pm, Sat/Sun 8.30am–5pm | admission and guided tour 216 rand. 320 km/200 miles from Bloemfontein*

(5 rooms | tel. 05 82 56 10 17 | www.pachamplace.co.za | Moderate); for dinner *Clementines* restaurant comes highly recommended *(Church Street | tel. 05 82 56 16 16 | Moderate)*. 280 km (175 miles) from Bloemfontein

GOLDEN GATE HIGHLANDS NATIONAL PARK ★ ⬩⬩ (136 C2) (*Ø K5*)

The park owes its name to the spectacular sandstone cliffs that shimmer gold when the sun catches them. Made up of

Interesting small shops: Windmill Centre in the artistic community of Clarens

CLARENS (136 C2) (*Ø K5*)

This village is a little jewel and the perfect place to stop over on your way to the national park. The inhabitants are predominantly Afrikaans, artists or both. Village life is best witnessed in the small galleries on Main Street or from the *Clarens Brewery* accompanied by a pint or two of its tasty craft beer. Spend the night at the friendly B&B *Patcham Place*

an area of 46 miles² in the rolling foothills of the Maluti Mountains, it is home to local game and there are also eagles that nest high up in the mountains.

There are two overnight camps in the park where you can rent a rondavel or cottage and, for higher standards, a hotel, the *Golden Gate Hotel (54 rooms | Moderate)*. *R 49 between Bethlehem and Harrismith | tel. 05 82 55 10 00 | 300 km*

(188 miles) from Bloemfontein | admission 176 rand

LADYBRAND (136 B–C2) (*ₒₒ J5*)

Located right on the Lesotho border this town in the middle of nowhere is surrounded by the majestic *Maluti Mountains.* It is characterised by old sandstone houses that line its exceptionally wide streets. Ladybrand was founded in 1867 as an Afrikaner defence post against the Basotho. Today this town enjoys extensive (and peaceful) trade with its Lesotho neighbours. The best overnight stop can be found in an old train station, seemingly desolated at first glance: The INSIDERTIP ▶ *Living Life Station House (5 rooms | 1 Princess Street | tel. 05 19 24 28 34 | Budget)* is an unexpectedly nice guesthouse with an 🌐 eco-café – the staff and the products are 100 per cent local!

LESOTHO ★

(136–137 B–D 2–3) (*ₒₒ J–K 5–6*)

This independent kingdom in the midst of mountain country is about the size of Belgium. Home to the Basotho since the beginning of the 19th century, the "roof of Africa" has a magnificent landscape but is still very underdeveloped in terms of a tourist infrastructure. The political unrest in the kingdom has done nothing to improve this situation. On a positive note, the country changed their national flag in 2006 and replaced the warrior symbols with the traditional pointed straw hat, the *mokorotlo.* Four-wheel drive motorists rejoice in the *Sani-Pass,* the mother of all passes: this 9 km/5.5 mile steep gravel path winds up the mountain to a height of 2874 m/9430 ft. The Aids project hotel 🌐 *Kick4Life (12 rooms | Nightingale Road | tel. 0 02 66 28 32 07 07 | www.kickforlife.org | Budget)* offers attractive accommodation in a good cause

in *Maseru;* the ⛰ *Malealea Lodge (54 rooms | tel. 08 25 52 42 15 | Budget–Moderate)* lies in an isolated valley in the western part of the country and offers hut accommodation with breath-taking views. The lodge has been committed to rescuing the village from poverty by employing local inhabitants. It is also the ideal base for pony trekking into the mountains *(from Maseru via Motsekuoa to Malealea). 150 km/112 miles from Bloemfontein*

WELKOM (136 B1) (*ₒₒ J4*)

Welkom is the pulse of the goldfields. The fact that this town was planned on the drawing board is still evident today. There are no traffic lights, very few stop streets – plenty of roundabouts. *Siete's Restaurant (Rovers Club | 58 Tempest Road | tel. 05 73 52 65 39 | Budget)* is very popular. An exciting adventure is a day tour of a gold mine. Tours must be booked in advance through *Welkom Tourism (tel. 05 73 52 92 44).* Welkom is also home to numerous bird species with flamingos visible in the *Flamingo Lake* outside the town. *150 km (94 miles) from Bloemfontein*

LOW BUDGET

Attention cowboys and -girls: All-inclusive horseback riding through a nature reserve in the mountain range bordering Lesotho: for as little as 2500 rand for two days. You will stay in a mountain hut overnight. Your bedding and provisions are carried by an off-road vehicle. *Bokpoort Farm near Clarens | tel. 0837444245 | www.bokpoort.com*

KWAZULU-NATAL

Admittedly, the country of South Africa has a varied landscape, yet the province of Kwa-Zulu-Natal is a microcosm in itself, in which Mowgli, Robinson Crusoe and even Reinhold Messner would feel at home.

The province is an eclectic melting pot of European, African and Asian cultures. The Africans are inextricably linked with King Shaka, the most powerful Zulu monarch of all time who was extremely influential in KZN as the South Africans refer to the Zulu Kingdom. The presence of kings usually means war and the Zulus furiously attacked the first Voortrekker who attempted to settle here. However the Boers were quick to take revenge and defeated the Zulu armies at the Battle of Blood River, declaring the Boer Republic but by 1843 the province was already under British control.

DURBAN

(137 E3) (_∏_ L6) The Zulu name for Durban (pop. 600,000) is Thekwini and means "the quiet lagoon". Durban is where South Africans choose to spend their holiday; the sea is warm and a mesmerizing shade of blue while the beaches are snowy white.

The sun shines here for 300 days a year and visitors to this vibrant port city will find it hard to believe that as recently 150 years ago there was nothing here but a wild jungle teeming with elephants.

Photo: Lighthouse on the beach at Umhlanga Rocks

For everyone who likes the sea nice and warm — the province on the Indian Ocean can be visited all year round

CITY **WHERE TO START?**
To the ● **Golden Mile,** a 6 km (3.7 mile) long beach promenade on the Marine Parade. It starts at the uShaka Marine World and takes you past Moses Mabhida Stadium to the Suncoast Casino. There are many parking spaces in the area.

At the end of 1497 Vasco da Gama came across this piece of paradise while en route to Asia. As it was on Christmas he called it Natal, the Portuguese word for Christmas. It was only in 1835 that it was renamed Durban after Sir Benjamin D'Urban, who was governor of the Cape in the mid 19th century. Many of Durban's inhabitants are descendants of the workforce that the then colonial British rulers brought in from India to tend the sugar plantations. Durban's Indian markets, mosques and stores are among Durban's attractions. Its harbour is South Africa's largest and it is the heartbeat of the city.

Souvenirs for the catwalk back home: beaded dresses from the Zulu collection in Durban

SIGHTSEEING

INSIDER TIP HARE KRISHNA TEMPLE OF UNDERSTANDING

Nowhere else outside India is more Indian than the district of Chatsworth. Nice temple with an excellent vegetarian restaurant. *Daily 10am–1pm, 4pm–8pm | admission free | 50 Bhaktivedanta Swami Circle | Chatsworth*

MOSES MABHIDA STADIUM ★

The most beautiful of the stadiums built for the 2010 Soccer World Cup. A 106 m (347 ft) high arch spans the stadium. Visitors can walk across it *(admission 90 rand)* or take the glassed-in cable car *(admission 60 rand)* The adventurous can swing through the stadium on a rope: the *Big Rush,* for 695 rand. *Daily 9am–5pm*

USHAKA MARINE WORLD ●

This aquarium and marine theme park has a distinctly Disneyland feel to it, only with Zulu huts and marimba. On display are more than 1000 fish species in elaborately designed aquariums. Dolphin shows are a classic: snorkelling or shark diving in the aquarium are much cooler. *Daily 9am–5pm | admission 146 rand | 1 Bell Road*

FOOD & DRINK

CAFÉ 1999

Small, all-in-white bistro – the highlight is the food on the plate. Casual dining at its best. *117 Vause Road | Berea | Tel. 03 12 02 34 06 | Moderate*

CIRCUS CIRCUS BEACH CAFE RESTAURANT

What a location! Directly on the beach, just a stone's throw away from the sea, this restaurant serves local, seasonal and fresh ingredients. Reserve a spot under one of their colourful parasols. *Snell Parade | tel. 0 31 33 77 00 | www.circuscircus. co.za | Budget*

THE LITTLE INDIA RESTAURANT
There is tough competition in Durban when it comes to naming the city's best curry and *Bunny Chows* (toast bread filled with curry). This restaurant definitely deserves to be ranked among the top 10; you can spend hours tasting your way through its delicious menu under the romantic lighting outside. *155 Musgrave Road | tel. 03 12 0 11 22 | www.littleindia arestaurant.co.za | Budget*

SHOPPING

AFRICAN ART CENTRE
Colourful and cheery: Arts and crafts by Zulu artists. *94 Florida Road | www.afri art.org.za*

I HEART MARKET
Every first Saturday in the month, the most creative and culinary-talented Durbanites display their goods which you will feel compelled to buy on the spot. *Imbizo Lawns, Moses Mabhida Stadium | www.iheartmarket.blogspot.co.za*

LEISURE & SPORTS

Cycling or skilfully skateboarding down the Golden Mile is great fun. A wet alternative is to surf or stand-up paddle. All equipment can be found at *Xpression on the Beach (tel. 07 41 34 12 32 | www. xpressiononthebeach.com)*. The *Giba Gorge Mountain Bike Park (admission 10–60 rand | 110 Stockville Road | Pinetown | www.gibagorge.co.za)* is perfect for a day trip with a picnic basket.

ENTERTAINMENT

MOYO USHAKA BAR ●
No better spot for a sundowner. Designer bar on the uShaka Pier only a few feet above the breakers. *1 Bell Street*

MUSGRAVE ROOF TOP MARKET
Markets are the new bars. Head to the 5th storey of this car park to try tasty grub from the street food stalls, listen to live music and post a selfie to show what a great time you're having. *Every last Fri in the month | Musgrave Centre | Berea*

WHERE TO STAY

INSIDER TIP ▶ **THE CONCIERGE**
While the façades remain intact, the interior of these four listed bungalows was overhauled by two design teams to exude modern luxury. The best address in trendy Morningside. Breakfast comes from the adjoining hipster café. *12 rooms | 37–43 St Mary's Av. | tel. 03 13 09 44 34 | www.the-concierge.co.za | Moderate*

GARDEN COURT MARINE PARADE ☆
Durban's beach skyline is dominated by huge concrete skyscrapers. No better on the outside than its neighbours, this hotel's interior is highly acclaimed and has amazing sea view windows.

⭐ **Moses Mabhida Stadium**
An architectural success – right on the Indian Ocean → p. 74

⭐ **Umhlanga Rocks**
The first choice for blonde beach babes → p. 77

⭐ **Valley of a Thousand Hills**
Magnificent views of undulating hills and valleys → p.77

⭐ **Drakensberg**
South Africa's "Alps"– an experience not just for mountaineers and hikers → p. 79

MARCO POLO HIGHLIGHTS

352 rooms | 167 Marine Terminal Street | tel. 03 13 37 33 41 | www.tsogosun.com/ garden-court-marine-parade | Expensive

QUARTERS ON FLORIDA

Superbly run hotel. The charming rooms come with bouquets of flowers and homemade biscuits. *25 rooms | 101 Florida Road | Morningside | tel. 03 13 03 52 46 | www.quarters.co.za | Expensive*

INFORMATION

DURBAN TOURISM

90 Florida Road | tel. 03 13 22 41 64 | www.durbanexperience.co.za

Stroll along the beach in the iSimangaliso Wetland Park

WHERE TO GO

HLUHLUWE-IMFOLOZI PARK
(137 F1–2) (*L–M4*)

This is the only place in KwaZulu-Natal where you will get to see the *Big Five* and of course other Savanna wild animals. In existence since 1895 and covering an area of 960 km²/370 miles², this stunning game reserve is South Africa's oldest in existence. *Daily Nov–Feb 5am–7pm, March–Oct 6am–6pm | admission 210 rand | 240 km (150 miles) from Durban*

ISIMANGALISO WETLAND PARK
(137 F1) (*M4*)

Boasting five ecosystems – lakes, ocean, dunes, savannah and wetlands – this park stretches along the Indian Ocean coast and has been declared a Unesco World Heritage site *(daily 6am–6pm | admission 50 rand per person and 55 rand per car)*. In the north of the park, 360 km (225 miles) from Durban is the **INSIDER TIP** *Thonga Beach Lodge (24 rooms | tel. 03 54 74 14 73 | www.thonga beachlodge.co.za | Expensive)*. Guests get to stay on an isolated stretch of beach in luxurious thatched rondavels.

SWAZILAND
(133 E–F 4–5) (*L–M 3–4*)

This tiny mountain country 500 km (313 miles) north of Durban is the world's last absolute monarchy, a fact which King Mswati III does not like to hear because it (rightly) puts him in a bad light. His subjects are unbelievably friendly and welcome you into their villages to stay in one of the ⊘ eco lodges spread across the country. One of these is the **INSIDER TIP** *Sobantu Guest Farm (3 rooms | at Piggs Peak | tel. 0026 86 05 39 54 | www.swa ziplace.com/sobantu | Budget)* near the Maguga dam. Information on the national parks at *www.biggameparks.org*.

Giraffes in Hluhluwe-Imfolozi Park, Africa's oldest wildlife reserve

UMHLANGA ROCKS ★
(137 E3) (*M L5*)

A contrast to the poor Swaziland. Only the rich and beautiful stay here in accommodation such as the ☀ *Oysterbox Hotel (86 rooms | 2 Lighthouse Road | tel. 03 15 14 50 00 | www.oysterboxhotel. com | Expensive)*. A slightly more down-to-earth alternative but with the same closeness to the sea is *Ballito* approx. 30 km/18 miles further north. The ☀ *Zimbali View Eco Guesthouse (5 rooms | 47 David Place | tel. 08 32 52 15 75 | www. zimbaliview.co.za | Moderate)* is located at the Dolphin Coast, a popular destination for, you've guessed it, dolphins.

VALLEY OF A THOUSAND HILLS ★ ☀
(137 E2–3) (*M L5*)

Your best view of the expansive, undulating hills and valleys is from Botha's Hill. *Information: 1000 Hills Tourism | tel. 03 17 77 18 74 | www.1000hills.kzn.org.*

za. Watch traditional Zulu dancing at the *Phezulu Safari Park (daily 8.30am– 4.30pm | admission 120 rand)*. *30 km (18 miles) from Durban*

PIETER-MARITZBURG

(137 E2) (*M L5*) **Tucked into one of the valleys of a thousand hills stands Pietermaritzburg (pop. 250,000) surrounded by a gently rolling hillside.**

The town has more Victorian buildings than anywhere else in South Africa. If you don't come to Pietermaritzburg for its history, then for the sport: The *Comrades Marathon* ends here and the world's largest open water swimming event, the *Midmar Mile,* takes place just around the corner.

LOW BUDGET

If you're not interested in visiting the uShaka Marine World in Durban, but are not immune to free entertainment, walk from the car park to Village Walk where you'll find restaurants, shops and relaxing walkways around the sea life pools.

SIGHTSEEING

OLD PRISON/PROJECT GATEWAY
The site where political prisoners were once tortured has been transformed into a social outreach organised by young people. NGO employees guide visitors through the prison museum and its social care program. *Mon–Fri 8am–4pm, Sat/Sun upob request | admission 20 rand | tel. 03 38 45 04 00 | 4 Burger Street*

TATHAM ART GALLERY ●
Not just a good address when it rains. A significant collection of contemporary South African art as well as some international and European masters. *Commercial Roadd | Tue–Sun 9am–5pm | admission free*

FOOD & DRINK

THE CAFE AT ROSEHURST
Light, fresh meals and delicious home baked rye bread. *239 Boom Street | tel. 03 33 94 38 83 | Budget*

OLIVE AND OIL
The Greek family who owns the restaurant brings a touch of the Mediterranean to the Indian Ocean. Olives, oil and seafood are all served in generous portions.

23 Mc Carthy Drive | tel. 03 33 47 11 31 | Moderate

WHERE TO STAY

FORDOUN HOTEL & SPA ●
On the outskirts of the city is Fordoun, one of South Africa's best spas. The *sangoma* or traditional healer prepares oils and tinctures from some 120 plants found in the gardens. Every room is uniquely furnished. *20 rooms | Nottingham Road | tel. 03 32 66 62 17 | www.fordoun.com | Expensive*

INFORMATION

PIETERMARITZBURG TOURISM
177 Chief Albert Luthuli Street | tel. 03 33 45 13 48 | www.pmbtourism.co.za

WHERE TO GO

DRAKENSBERG ★

(136–137 C–E 1–3) *(🕮 J–L 4–6)*

The Drakensberg is the highest massif in southern Africa. The view you get of the northern Drakensberg from the *Royal Natal National Park* is breathtaking – before you in all its glory is the rock face called the Amphitheatre. Nestled in a spectacular setting, the *Montusi Mountain Lodge (16 cottages | Bergville | tel. 03 64 38 62 43 | www.montusi.co.za | Expensive)* offers fantastic views of the mountains. An absolute must if you're not afraid of heights is the trek up the approx. 3000 m/9842 ft high *Sentinel Peak* (starting at approx. 2500 m/8200 ft). You will need to climb up a vertical 40 m/130 ft high steel ladder to reach the top. En route to the neighbouring *Kamberg Nature Reserve* you will find the small INSIDER TIP *Cleopatra Mountain Farmhouse (11 rooms | tel. 03 32 67 72 43 | www.cleopatramountain.com | Expensive)* hotel with bags of retro charm. Guests are treated to a select menu cooked by the owners every evening – and they know what they are doing. *100 km (63 miles) from Pietermaritzburg*

INSIDER TIP MIDLANDS MEANDER

(137 D2) *(🕮 K5)*

The picturesque area surrounding *Nottingham Road* is an artists' haven. Some 150 artists, craftsmen and restaurants form part of the 80 km (50 mile) route between Pietermaritzburg and Mooi River and are open to the general public to visit. Well signposted, participating galleries and studios are easy to find to the right and left of the N 3.

The green hills of Africa: Cathedral Peak Valley in the Drakensberg massif

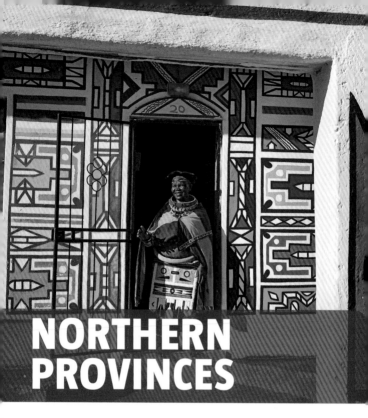

NORTHERN PROVINCES

When you jet into Johannesburg International Airport in the morning you know you have arrived in Africa: the dry Highveld air, the reddish steppe-like grasslands that seem to go on forever, the bright blue sky and the breathtakingly beautiful sunrise.

The north was the last part of South Africa that the white settlers colonised. Johannesburg is only just over 130 years old, while neighbouring Pretoria only a few decades older. The northern provinces (the Orange Free State and Transvaal) were founded by the Voortrekkers who fled from the Cape and the British in the mid 19th century. No sooner were diamonds discovered and the British wanted to convince their former opponents to enter into a confederation with them. When this failed, they annexed the republics. This sparked the beginning of the first Anglo-Boer War or *Vryheidsoorlog* as it is known in Afrikaans. The Boers were the victors in this dispute. When a huge gold discovery was made near Pretoria in 1886 they were well aware of the problems that it would bring with it. The discovery could not be kept secret and the resultant gold rush attracted thousands of fortune seekers from around the world.

The British had become resolute in their intention to capture this part of southern Africa for themselves. The Second Boer War broke out with Britain emerging victorious in 1902. In 1910 the South African Republic was founded – with Pretoria as its administrative capital. Pre-

Photo: traditional house in the Mpumalanga province

The former Transvaal is the economic heart-beat of South Africa thanks to the cities Johannesburg and Pretoria

toria is still the administrative capital even today although many see the city as Johannesburg's little sister. The area where the gold was discovered is called the Witwatersrand. It is a 1700 m (5577 ft) high plateau with a gold-bearing vein that stretches for more than 130 km (80 miles) widening to 30 km (18 miles) to-wards the end it. It is an area of mining and industrial towns – the largest being Johannesburg which is the economic powerhouse in the south of Africa.

On a road trip to the north, you pass through hilly grassland terrain to Warm-bath (Bela-Bela). The locals called it the "boiling place" because of its hot springs that erupt from the ground here at 53 de-grees Celsius. From here the road takes you hundreds of kilometres via the Wa-terberg region and Polokwane through baobab terrain across the Soutpansberg Mountains to the Limpopo River (that forms the border to Zimbabwe and Bot-swana). Travelling through this unspoilt part of Africa is an unforgettable expe-rience. Only recently some very rare plants and birds were discovered in a valley of the isolated Venda Mountains. The most interesting province in the north has to be Mpumalanga. Here settlers discovered gold before the rush began on the Witwatersrand. Tiny Pilgrim's not been fully explored but it is home to Sun City – known as the Las Vegas of South Africa – and two massive nature reserves: Pilansberg and Madikwe. Both are popular attractions with Johannesburg locals because they are in easy driving

Lights still on in Sandton: Johannesburg's skyline at night

Rest was pivotal to the early gold rush and today it is a living museum, a listed town and a tourist attraction where you can try your luck with the gold pan. What makes this province so impressive are its countless lookout points with views over its bizarre landscape and spectacular waterfalls. The inland plateau experiences a dramatic drop to a subtropical level, a landscape of misty mountains and waterfalls. One particular lookout point along the Blyde River Canyon, not to be missed on the way to or from the Kruger National Park, is the appropriately named *God's Window*. From here you get to look down 700 m/2296 ft onto the canyon below. North West Province is one of the poorest provinces and its tourism potential has distance. Said to be one hundred times older than the Himalayas, the Magaliesberg Mountains with its fertile valleys are also accessible for a weekend getaway.

JOHANNES-BURG

MAP ON P. 138/139
(132 C4) *(ω J–K3)* Johannesburg is South Africa's largest city (pop. 4.5 million) and goes by various names including Joburg, Jozi, eGoli (the latter due to the gold rush). Johannesburg's problem is its reputation, perhaps un-

deservedly so; statistically speaking, there are fewer homicides here than in Cape Town and the city's regeneration has placed it on the map of insider places to visit among hip young travellers.

Their inevitable rivals from Cape Town describe life in Johannesburg as hectic and chaotic; a comment smirked at by visiting Europeans. One thing is sure: there is more Africa in Johannesburg than anywhere else in South Africa. Since it was founded in 1886, the city has attracted people from all over the world, first from Europe, and since the end of the apartheid, from other African countries. Just like the gold diggers before them, people come to Johannesburg today looking to make their fortune. The metropolis is the country's commercial and financial capital and home of the stock exchange, the largest airport, the widest roads and the highest skyscrapers – and since the 2010 World Cup it also has the high speed *Gautrain* that takes commuters from Sandton to the airport in less than 15 minutes. During the apartheid era, Sandton became the new more palatable residential and commercial hub while the old historic centre became increasingly run down. However that has changed in recent years and today downtown is considered cool again. During the day it is the workplace of bankers and mine industry employees while in the evening districts are taken over by students, artists and creative thinkers.

The contrasts that have gained the city a reputation as South Africa's capital of crime are visible on every corner: tailor-made suits and designer shoes in the latest luxurious restaurants in front of which lie beggars next to traffic lights. Cardboard boxes serve as beds in dark alleyways while high-security walls and electric fences guard luxury properties in the northern suburbs. One new busi-

🏙 WHERE TO START?

Hop on and off – the red buses can be seen everywhere but in Johannesburg they offer you the perfect introduction to the city. Hop on at **Park Station Downtown** or the Rosebank Mall in the north, hop off at the Carlton Centre for the view, a stroll in Newtown and Braamfontein. *www.citysightseeing.co.za*

ness skyscraper after the next is popping up in the affluent districts of Rosebank and Sandton while most of the houses in the neighbouring townships are still built with corrugated iron walls. The list goes on and on. Yet despite these juxtapositions, Johannesburg is an extremely friendly and unstuffy city. No wonder since the city has seen such an influx of people since the first gold rush. Nobody

MARCO POLO HIGHLIGHTS

⭐ Soweto
On a tour through the township you begin to understand what apartheid meant for the people → p. 85

⭐ Sun City
Luxury entertainment oasis with hotels and casinos → p. 88

⭐ Union Buildings
The seat of government in Pretoria is at its best in October when the jacarandas are in bloom → p. 89

⭐ Kruger National Park
The world's most famous game reserve → p. 90

is a stranger here. And one other fact: Johannesburg is the only city of its massive size in the world which is not located near a major source of water. It has however developed from a dusty tent camp to a thriving metropolis.

Old Fort Prison, where Nelson Mandela served part of his time behind bars. In contrast to previous court buildings it is friendly, warm, open to the general public and filled with contemporary art. The tour through the prison is an in-

Apartheid Museum – for an in-depth look at South Africa's political past

SIGHTSEEING

APARTHEID MUSEUM (0) (🗺 0)
Black? white? coloured? This often randomly designated distinction ruined lives and is still not easy for society to shake off. This huge, contemporary museum is well done; you should plan a few hours for your visit and know that you can't see everything. *Northern Parkway | Gold Reef Road | daily 9am–5pm | admission 80 rand*

CONSTITUTION HILL (143 D2) (🗺 0)
South Africa's new Constitutional Court has been built next to the notorious

tensive experience; a stroll around the old fort is a welcome relief afterwards with its views over the city. *Corner Hospital Street/11 Kotze Street | daily 9am–5pm | various guided tours through prison, court and museum, e.g. at night or as "time travel" | admission 65 rand*

GOLD REEF CITY (0) (🗺 0)
Across from the Apartheid Museum is the entertainment park with casino where you can enjoy the more fun things in life. An interesting *Underground Tour* takes you down the mine shafts of this former gold mine. *Daily 9.30am–5pm |*

M 1 South motorway, exit Gold Reef City |
www.tsogosun.com/gold-reef-city-casino

SOWETO ⭐ (0) (📖 0)

Taxis beeping their horns, house music pounding out of run-down shacks – you've come to the wrong place if you're looking for peace. But this is Soweto, an address of pride for its inhabitants, with an eclectic and vibrant street life that puts the deserted alleys and metre-high fences in the northern suburbs in a dull light. Soweto stands for *South Western Townships,* a conglomeration of settlements which today is home to around four million people. The city's grim past collides with its optimistic future on the famous Vilakazi Street in Orlando West. A tour will first take you to the *Hector Pieterson Museum (8287 Khumalo Road | daily 10am–5pm | admission 30 rand)* close by. It was founded in memory of a 14-year old school boy who was shot by the police during a demonstration with hundreds of other pupils against the apartheid regime. The walk to the restaurants and coffee shops at the end of Vilakazi Street takes you past the former homes of two recipients of the Noble Peace Prize: Desmond Tutu and Nelson Mandela. Tutu's house is a private home while visitors can journey back to the Fifties in the *Mandela House (8115 Vilakazi Street | daily 9am–5pm | admission 60 rand)* to the time when Tata Madiba – as Mandela is lovingly known to South Africans – resided here. *Moafrika Tours (www.sowetotour.co.za)* offers various tours of the township.

And while only a handful of tourists would have been courageous enough to go to the township by armoured bus a decade ago, it's now so safe to visit that many are venturing there by bike. Lebo and his Swedish wife Maria started organising INSIDER TIP bike tours *(2 or 4 hours | 470–580 rand | sowetobackpackers.co.za)* in the early 2000s, offering local guides the chance to show visitors what life is really like in the township. The tour is a touching and authentic experience. Food will be provided but don't forget the sun cream!

FOOD & DRINK

CHAF POZI (0) (📖 0)

Shiza Nyama (barbecued meat with polenta and Chakalaka salad) is the finger-licking speciality of this restaurant at the foot of the graffiti-sprayed Orlando Towers. A quiet spot during the week but full on weekends. Kwaito beats played by the DJ. *Closed Mon/Tue | corner of Chris Hani and Nicolas Street | tel. 08 17 97 57 56 | www.chafpozi.co.za | Budget*

INSIDER TIP THE LOCAL GRILL (0) (📖 0)

South Africa is the land of the carnivores. Even the unhappiest cows in South Africa have it far better than their European counterparts – and you can taste the difference. Manager Steven knows everything there is to know about beef; his *Beef Appreciation* courses are cowtastic. *40 7th Av. Parktown North | tel. 01 08 80 19 46 | Moderate*

MARBLE (0) (📖 0)

The city's sleekest restaurant. Its design alone is worth the visit, but you do pay extra for it. All types of quality, aromatic ingredients are cooked on a grand wood-fired grill. The 🍸 bar attracts the coolest of crowds and offers fantastic views over the green hillside to the north of Joburg. The entire Trumpet building is one giant work of artistic architecture. *Corner of Keyes and Jellicoe Av. | tel. 01 05 94 55 50 | www.marble. restaurant | Expensive*

MOYO (0) (*ɸ 0*)

An open air venue next to Zoo Lake that serves traditional African dishes in an ethnic atmosphere. Ideal spot for lunch. *1 Prince of Wales Drive | tel. 0116 46 00 58 | Moderate*

SHOPPING

BRYANSTON ORGANIC MARKET ⊗ (0) (*ɸ 0*)

A fun meeting point for the organically minded and a fixed date in the calendar for eco-conscious Joburgers for the last 40 years. *Thu and Sat 9am–3pm | 40 Culross Road | www.bryanstonorganicmarket.co.za*

MABONENG PRECINCT
(139 F4–5) (*ɸ 0*)

Young investors have overhauled a former no-go area into an impressively creative centre, making it a firm favourite with the international backpacker scene. Open on Sundays, it offers great street food in the *Arts-on-Main* complex, craft beer by *Smack! Republic* and many vibrant shops and bars to be explored around Commissioner and Fox Street. *www.mabonengprecinct.com*

ROSEBANK SUNDAY MARKET
(0) (*ɸ 0*)

African, original and homemade items can all be found on the rooftop of the *Rosebank Mall* car park. With over 200 market and food stalls to browse around, time flies up here. *Last Sunday of the month 9am–4pm | 50 Bath Av. | www.rosebanksundaymarket.co.za*

ENTERTAINMENT

MARKET THEATRE (138 B4) (*ɸ 0*)

A good address for high-quality theatre productions, usually presenting mod-

ern-day issues. The complex dedicated to the arts houses a bookstore, a gallery and a bar in what used to be the city's market hall. The *Newtown Junction Mall* offers parking and you can eat there before the show at *Potatoe Shed (tel. 0105 90 61 33 | Moderate)*. *56 Margaret Mcingana Street | tel. 0118 32 16 41*

THE ORBIT JAZZ CLUB & BISTRO
(138 B2) (*ɸ 0*)

A permanent fixture on the music scene in the lively district of Braamfontein. Attracting a diverse audience, the venue hosts live music, usually jazz in its many forms. *Closed Sun/Mon| 81 De Korte Street | tel. 0113 39 66 45 | www.theorbit.co.za*

INSIDER TIP SIN & TAXES (0) (*ɸ 0*)

A barkeeper is now a mixologist or so the master of cocktails Julian Short likes to call himself. His tiny, exclusively furnished bar is well hidden, which is all part of the experience. *Corner of Bolton and Jan Smuts Road | tel. 0109 00 49 87*

WHERE TO STAY

INSIDER TIP LUCKY BEAN GUESTHOUSE
(0) (*ɸ 0*)

Laid-back and intimate guesthouse. There is nobody better than owner Conway to recount tales of Melville district's alternative past. The comfortable rooms are surrounded by a garden of paradise. The ᵥᐧ *Skyline Suite*, of course, has the best views. *9 rooms | 129 1st Av. | Melville | tel. 0114 82 55 72 | Moderate*

NEO'S B & B (0) (*ɸ 0*)

Since Neo Mamashela lost her job in 2000, her mission has been to show guests her friendly neighbourhood of Soweto. *4 rooms | 8041 Bacela Street/ near Vilakazi Street | Orlando West | tel. 0115 36 04 13 | Budget*

Alternative, hip, vibrant and alive: the hipster district Maboneng Precinct

THE PEECH HOTEL 🌐 (0) (*📖 0*)
Six of the rooms in this stylish hotel in up-market Melrose have been designed to be environmentally friendly. Solar energy heats the water and wastewater is recycled in the garden. *16 rooms | 61 North Street | tel. 011 537 97 97 | www.thepeech. co.za | Expensive*

PROTEA HOTEL BY MARRIOTT PARKTONIAN 〽️ (138 C2) (*📖 0*)
A landmark on the Johannesburg skyline. If there were no rooms, you probably wouldn't object to camping out on the rooftop just to see this panoramic view. *300 rooms | 120 De Korte Street | Braamfontein | tel. 011 403 57 40 | www. marriott.com | Expensive*

TEN BOMPAS (0) (*📖 0*)
Each suite has been decorated by a different interior designer using various themes. They all have their own fireplace and steam bath. *10 rooms | 10 Bom-pas Road | Randburg | tel. 011 325 24 42 | www.tenbompas.com | Expensive*

GAUTENG TOURISM (138 D5) (*📖 0*)
124 Main Street | Marshalltown | tel. 011 085 25 00 | www.gauteng.net

JOBURG TOURISM (138 C3) (*📖 0*)
Park Station | tel. 011 338 50 51 | www. joburgtourism.com

WHERE TO GO

THE CRADLE OF HUMANKIND NATURE RESERVE ⬤ (132 C4) (*📖 J3*)
The beginnings of humankind can be traced here. The Unesco World Heritage Site comprises several fossil sites, the oldest of which, *Little Foot,* is around 3 million years old. A new, extinct species of humankind was only discovered deep underground in 2015: the homo naledi. Vis-

itors can explore various parts of the *Cradle,* the *Maropeng Visitor Centre (www.maropeng.co.za)* and the *Sterkfontein Caves*. A combined entrance costs 190 rand. Great lunch after your visit can be had at *Roots Restaurant (Letamo Game Estate | tel. 0116 68 70 00 | www.forum homini.com | Moderate)*.

SUN CITY ★ (132 B3) (*ⓜ J3*)

About two-and-a-half hours and a 160 km (100 mile) drive from Johannesburg, South Africa's answer to Las Vegas, *Sun City,* looms out of the barren landscape like an oasis in a desert. MAybe Fata Morgana is more fitting: four monumental hotels, an amusement park with a lake and two top-notch golf courses appear out of nowhere. Everything you see – rocks, waterfalls, palms or flamingos – is either artificial or imported.

The business magnate Sol Kerzner opened his entertainment palace in 1979 with casino, shows and restaurants and went on to expand it over the years. This complex stands as a testimony to the double moral standards of the apartheid state. Sun City was built in a homeland, declared an independent state by the apartheid government, so it could provide entertainment such as gambling which was otherwise banned in "white" states. There was no form of racial segregation because the venue brought in revenue. Sun City even has its own airport where flights from Johannesburg land daily. A shuttle service ferries guests from the car park at the entrance to the entertainment venues. The hotels in Sun City itself cater for every budget and taste. Families may prefer the *Cabanas (380 rooms | Expensive)* while those who like luxury and kitsch should opt for *The Palace of the Lost City (335 rooms | Moderate)*; for all the hotels on site: *tel. 0117 80 78 55 | www.suninternational.com)*.

PRETORIA

(132 C4) (*ⓜ J–K3*) **Today amalgamated with the metropolitan municipality of Tshwane, Pretoria (pop. 3 million) is the province capital, yet people in Johannesburg are quick to poke fun at their conservative neighbours.**

Maybe the folk of Johannesburg are only giving out what they take from their rivals in Cape Town or maybe because Pretoria is indeed quieter and more reserved than the brash Joburg. But Pretoria has more Jacaranda trees, estimated at around 70,000. When they blossom in October, the city becomes a sea of lilac blue.

LOW BUDGET

Staying at a privately run game lodge can be expensive. An exception is the ⓦ *Mosetlha Bush Camp (9 rooms | tel. 0114 44 93 45 | www.thebushcamp.com)* in the Madikwe Game Reserve. An eco-lodge without electricity where you get to shower under the African skies – a terrific atmosphere and not disturbing nature too much.

Fancy a stroll around the *Johannesburg Art Gallery (corner at Klein and King George Street | Joubert Park | Tues–Sun 10am–5pm | free admission)*? It is largest art gallery in South Africa and its collection is so vast that the gallery can only exhibit a tenth of its works at one time. Housed in one of the last remaining historic downtown buildings, it was beautifully renovated in 2015.

SIGHTSEEING

UNION BUILDINGS ★

When architect Sir Herbert Baker built this majestic piece of architecture on Meintjieskop hill in 1910, he surely couldn't have guessed that 84 years later the first black president would have been inaugurated at the same site. After Mandela's death, his body was also transported to lie in state at the Union Buildings government headquarters where thousands of mourners queued up around the park grounds to see him.

VOORTREKKER MONUMENT

Inaugurated as a memorial and museum in 1949 in honour of the courageous Boers who emigrated with their ox carts from the Cape colony eastwards, this monument was for a long time seen by conservative Afrikaners as a symbol of their strength as a nation. Today, the hillside location of this overbearing monument is the venue for the

CITY **WHERE TO START?**
Burgerpark on Jacob Maré Street is a good place to set out from. Opposite is Melrose House and from here you can follow Andries Street until you get to Minaar Street and the Transvaal Museum. Opposite it is the city hall and a block away in Visagie Street is the Cultural History Museum surrounded by yet another park. Parking spaces can be found in Pretorius Street and the car parks along Francis Baard Street

peace-loving *Park Acoustics* music festival held once a month *(www.park acoustics.co.za)*. *Eufees Road | Groenkloof | May–Aug 8am–5pm, Sept–April 8am–6pm | admission 70 rand | www.vtm.org.za*

Flowers in front of the government headquarters at Union Buildings

FOOD & DRINK

INSIDER TIP FERMIER

Not content with just serving local and seasonal ingredients, this restaurant even offers a nine-course menu which uses as much of the animal as possible. The concept restaurant by chef Adriaan Maree was constructed using leftover rubble from the area and the interior was designed by artisans from the Karoo Yard, a collective of artists next door. *Corner of Albeth and Lynwood Road | tel. 07 60 72 52 61 | Expensive*

LA TERRASSE ROOFTOP CAFÉ

North and South Africa meet here. Moroccan architecture, colours, spices and hospitality in the middle of a densely overgrown garden – delightful.*435 Atterbury Road | tel. 01 23 46 57 13 | www. moroccanhouse.co.za | Budget*

SHOPPING

INSIDER TIP ANTIQUE ROUTE 6

There are some hidden treasures to be found in Pretoria's antique shops. You will meet some curious characters and discover their collections on this easy to follow route through the historic centre. *www.antiqueroute6pretoria.co.za*

CINNAMON LIFESTYLE & DESIGN

Perfect if you need a souvenir to take back to somebody who already has everything. *Shop 6, Monument Park, Shopping Centre | 73 Skilpad Av.*

ENTERTAINMENT

CAPITAL CRAFT

Home-brewed, craft beers have exploded onto the market. Four friends decided to tap into this trend and launch the *Beer Academy*. In cool wooden and industrial furnishings, guests are invited to try over 200 kinds of wheat and hop creations, accompanied by good pub grub. *Greenlyn Village Centre, Shop No 20 | Lynwood | tel. 01 24 24 86 01*

WHERE TO STAY

ALPINE ATTITUDE HOTEL

Stylish and chic boutique hotel with lots of art, each of the rooms has a theme like the *African Room,* the *Transparent Room* or the *Nature Room. 7 rooms | 522 Atterbury Road | www.alpineattitude. co.za | Expensive*

INSIDER TIP ROSEMARY HILL

Home-grown vegetables, creatively recycled plastics, soaps and lotions using ingredients from the herbal garden and very comfortable rooms. This organic farm (20 min. away from Pretoria) is a pioneer in sustainability and social responsibility. *11 rooms | On the N4 eastbound | tel. 01 28 02 00 52 | www.rosemaryhill.co.za | Moderate*

INFORMATION

TSHWANE TOURISM ASSOCIATION
309 Church Square | tel. 01 23 58 14 30 | www.tshwanetourism.co.za | www.go pretoria.co.za

WHERE TO GO

KRUGER NATIONAL PARK ★
(133 E–F 1–3) (ጠ L–M 1–3)
Almost everyone has heard of this wild park – and rightly so. No other park in Africa can boast so many different species of animals. Covering an area roughly the size of Wales, you can meet 17,000 elephants, 48,000 buffalos, 1500 lions and 1000 leopards – or none at all. Depending on your luck.

Did you know? The Kruger National Park is also home to tigers

There are nine entry gates into the park. You can reach five of these from *Nelspruit* on the N4; *Malelane, Crocodile Bridge, Phabeni, Numbi* and the *Paul Kruger Gate*. Approximately halfway up the park there are the *Orpen* and *Phalabora* gates, while the *Punda Maria* and *Pafuri* gates are right up in the north. There are endless offers of accommodation in the park from bush tents, huts and houses to luxury lodges. Self-catering or all-inclusive packages are offered, as are "on foot" safaris and private rangers. The bigger ones like *Bergendahl* or *Satara* have restaurants and even swimming pools. South Africa realised the need for nature conservation at an early stage. The Kruger National Park came about as a result of the government prohibiting hunting in the area between the Sabie and Crocodile Rivers way back in the 19th century. The roads in the park are good and there is an extensive network of both surfaced and unsurfaced roads and tracks to explore. Visitors drive through in their own vehicles and try to spot animals. The maximum speed on surfaced roads is 50 km/h (31 mph), on unsurfaced roads 40 km/h (25 mph) *(gates open Oct–March 5.30am, April–Sept 6am; gates close 5.30pm–6.30pm depending on the month | admission 304 rand | information and reservations: South African National Parks (tel. 012 428 91 11 | www.sanparks.co.za | 380 km (238 miles) from Pretoria).*

INSIDER TIP *The Outpost Lodge* on the border to neighbouring Zimbabwe and Mozambique is a private rest camp inside the Kruger National Park. The Makuleke tribe previously owned the land, were dispossessed of it when it became part of the park and then reclaimed it in the 1990s. The tribe received a concession for a private lodge to be built on the land. *The Outpost (12 rooms | tel. 011 327 39 10 | www.seasonsinafrica.com | Moderate)* offers the ultimate in luxury and beauty: a completely open plan space with uninterrupted views of the wilderness around.

If you prefer not to stay over in the Kruger National Park rest camps or at the more expensive private reserves then the *Graskop Hotel (36 rooms | tel. 013 767 12 44 | www.graskophotel.co.za | Moderate)* in Graskop is a good option. Owner Harrie collects art and some of the hotel rooms are decorated with works by famous South African artists.

MPUMALANGA
(133 D–E 3–4) (*ⅅ K–L 2–4*)

This province is predominantly subtropical with fertile plains. On the ⬚ *Panorama Route* you will have unparalleled views of typical African forests and savannah. The *Blue Jay Lodge (5 rooms | tel. 013 737 75 46 | www.bluejaylodge. co.za | Expensive)* is one of the best en route. Guests are treated as family.

You will find some of the country's most beautiful private game parks in this province, one of which is *Thornybush Game Reserve.* The lodges are predictably expensive but you don't have to organise a thing and can sit back and enjoy the full safari experience. The *KwaMbili Game Lodge (5 rooms | tel. 0157 93 27 73 | www. kwambilisafarilodge.com | Expensive)* charges "entry-level" prices for its pretty tent rooms or houses.

Sabie is one of Mpumalanga larger cities. It is surrounded by dense forests and lots of waterfalls – the most well known is *Mac Mac Falls* 10 km (6 miles) away – and makes for a good starting point from which to set out to explore the scenic landscape of the *Blyde River Canyon,* a fascinating canyon towered over by cliffs resembling round huts. The canyon is 40 km (25 miles) from Sabie via *Graskop.* Get the best view from ⬚ *God's Window.*

Located only 20 minutes from Graskop is *Pilgrim's Rest,* a tiny village that is the

product of South Africa's first gold rush. In 1873 Alex Patterson came across the first gold nuggets in a small tributary of the Blyde River while traversing the land with a wheelbarrow. He tried unsuccessfully to keep his discovery a secret, and in no time at all there was an influx of some 1500 prospectors. First they settled in tents but soon corrugated iron houses, shops and bars sprung up and one of them – the INSIDER TIP Royal Hotel – still exists today *(50 rooms | Uptown Pilgrim's Rest | tel. 013 768 11 00 | Moderate).* A pleasurable experience for those who enjoy delving into the past..

Panning for gold came to an abrupt end after seven years and was replaced with underground mining when a company bought the mineral rights. The mine was finally shut down 100 years after that auspicious day when Patterson found his first nugget. Today *Pilgrim's Rest* is a listed outdoor museum. If you would like to try your luck then you too can also pan for gold. Find out more at

An accessible riverscape: Blyde River Canyon in Mpumalanga

the *Diggings Museum* at the town's entrance.

The entrance to *Mount Sheba Nature Reserve* is some 20 km (12.5 miles) from Pilgrim's Rest. The reserve does not have any big game; its main attraction is some 100 different tree species that are home to cavorting monkeys. The reserve is significant for its indigenous rain forest, making it a perfect ecosystem. Visitors wanting to explore the private reserve on foot have a choice of eleven hiking trails ranging from 1 km to 6 km (3.7 miles) *(admission free)*. However, visitors should register at the reception ot the *Mount Sheba Lodge (25 rooms | tel. 01 37 68 12 41 | www.mount-sheba. co.za | Expensive)*. The hotel is above the rainforest.

NORTH WEST PROVINCE
(132 A–C 3–5) (*Ø F–J 2–4*)

There are five good reasons to drive to the North West Province. Big Five reasons, to be precise. Tourists and locals alike who don't have time for the Kruger national park visit the province for its game reserves. One of the most well known is the *Pilanesberg Game Reserve (daily March/April 6am–6.30pm, May–Sept 6.30am–6pm, Oct 6am-6.30pm | admission 110 rand | an additional 40 rand vehicle charge | www.pilanesberg-nationalpark.org)* which is also easily accessible from Johannesburg, 230 km (144 miles) away. There are pretty lodges available and – the main advantage for families with small children – no malaria. Right in the north of North West Province is the INSIDER TIP *Madikwe Game Reserve*. It is an exclusive location as it is too far out of the way for day tourists. One of the most attractive of the reserve's 20 camps is the family-friendly *Motswiri Private Safari Lodge (tel. 011 3 63 35 87 | www.motswiri.com | Expensive)*. With only six straw-roofed bush villas available, you are given the feeling to be alone in the wilderness. With an all-round service guaranteed of course.

DISCOVERY TOURS

① SOUTH AFRICA AT A GLANCE

START: ① Johannesburg
END: ㉑ Cape Town

15 days
Driving time
(without stops)
approx. 55 hours

Distance:
➡ 3820 km/2374 miles

COSTS: approx. 38,750 rand for two people (incl. accommodation, food and drink, rental car, petrol etc.)
WHAT TO PACK: enough food and drinking water for each day of the tour

IMPORTANT TIPS: The journey by car can take longer than you'd maybe expect from the number of kilometres due to poor road or weather conditions.

Would you like to explore the places that are unique to this country? Then the Discovery Tours are just the thing for you – they include terrific tips for stops worth making, breathtaking places to visit, selected restaurants and fun activities. It's even easier with the touring App: download the tour with map and route to your smartphone using the QR Code on pages 2/3 or from the website address in the footer below – and you'll never get lost again even when you're offline. → p. 2/3

A journey across the country at the southernmost tip of Africa is a truly fantastic experience. This tour takes you through wildlife reserves and tropical forests, through picturesque mountain ranges and thrilling semideserts and along the ocean.

The commercial capital of the African continent, a city abuzz with boundless energy and drive, multiple lane motorways and wild motorists, skyscrapers and sprawling townships – that's ❶ Johannesburg → p. 82. But as soon as you leave the outskirts of this megacity **on the N 12 and then eastwards on the N 4,** you will have the

DAY 1

❶ Johannesburg

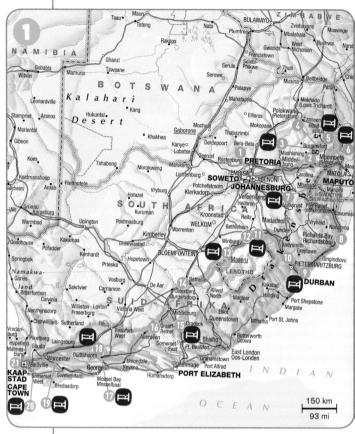

372 km / 231 mi
2 Sabie 🍴
30 km / 18.6 mi
☕
3 Graskop 🛏

great expanse of Africa ahead of you. Set off around 9am to avoid hitting the city's rush hour. **Exit the motorway at Nelspruit (Mbombela). Continue your journey along the famous _Panorama Route_ (R 539) to** **2** Sabie → p. 92, where you can eat lunch in the country inn **The Wild Fig Tree** _(34 Main Street | tel. 01 37 64 22 39 | Budget)_. From here it is only 15 km/9 miles to the **Mac Mac Falls**, where water cascades over 70 m/230 ft down to the depths below. The small town of **3** Graskop is a suitable place to spend your first night; **it is only 15 km/9 miles away along the R 532.** The nicest hotel around is the **Graskop Hotel** _(36 rooms | Hoof Street 3 | tel. 01 37 67 12 44 | www.graskop hotel.co.za | Budget)_.

Head off the next morning along the **R 532 and R 534** to the viewpoint ❹ **God's Window** → p. 92. The view over the Blyde River Canyon is breath-taking; the earlier you get there, the better. After spending two hours soaking up the magnificent mountain scenery, **head north and then east along the R 532 and R 531 respectively until you return to the R 40.** From here you'll reach the **Orpen Gate**, one of the entrances to the ❺ **Kruger National Park** → p. 90, one of the continent's largest and most spectacular wildlife reserves. Just a few kilometres past the entrance is the **Orpen Gate Rest Camp** (tel. 01 24 28 91 11 | www.sanparks.org | Budget), your self-catering accommodation for the night.

The next day begins at sunrise. Drive along the tarmac roads right into the wilderness of the Kruger Park passing by Africa's diverse wildlife to the **Malelane Gate** in the south of the reserve. You should plan a day for this trip. On leaving the park in ❻ **Malelane**, you can spend the night at the **Rio Vista Lodge** (Monte Vista Estate | tel. 01 37 90 12 46 | www.linoslodge.co.za | Moderate).

Your journey continues the next day along the R 570 to the small independent kingdom of ❼ **Swaziland** → p. 76. Guests at the hotel INSIDER TIP **Foresters Arms** (34 rooms | Mhlambanyatsi | tel. 0026 8 24 67 41 77 | www.forestersarms.co.za | Moderate), just 30 km/19 miles from the capital Mbabane, feel like in the film "Out of Africa". It's worth staying an extra day here to explore the surroundings by mountain bike (available from the hotel).

After two nights' stay in Swaziland, head back to South Africa **on the N 2 to the Indian Ocean.** The first stop is ❽ **St Lucia** in the **iSimangaliso Wetland Park** → p. 76. Try the fresh fish for lunch at the **Braza Restaurant** (McKenzie Street | tel. 03 55 90 12 42 | Moderate), while watching the hippopotamuses and crocodiles in the water just 100 m/330 ft away. This is as good as safari can get. **From the wetlands, drive on the N 2 southbound.** This stretch of the coast is relatively untouched by tourism and offers fantastic scenery. The pulsating metropolis of ❾ **Durban** → p. 72 in the Kwa-Zulu-Natal province couldn't be more different. If price isn't an issue, then the **Oysterbox Hotel** is the place to stay at the bathing resort of **Umhlanga Rocks** → p. 77 on the Indian Ocean.

The long stretch of sand in front of the hotel invites you to take a morning stroll **before leaving Durban on the**

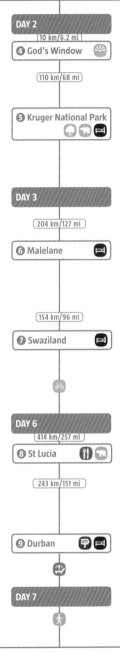

DAY 2

10 km/6.2 mi

❹ God's Window

110 km/68 mi

❺ Kruger National Park

DAY 3

204 km/127 mi

❻ Malelane

154 km/96 mi

❼ Swaziland

DAY 6

414 km/257 mi

❽ St Lucia

243 km/151 mi

❾ Durban

DAY 7

141 km/88 mi

⑩ Midlands Meander

268 km/167 mi

⑪ Golden Gate Highlands National Park

DAY 8

35 km/22 mi

⑫ Clarens

148 km/92 mi

⑬ Ladybrand

DAY 9

331 km/206 mi

⑭ Gariep Dam

217 km/135 mi

⑮ Cradock

DAY 10–11

138 km/86 mi

⑯ Graaff-Reinet

N 3 again to the enchanted Natal Midlands. On the so-called ⑩ **Midlands Meander** → p. 79 between Pietermaritzburg and Mooi River, you will find several artists and craftsmen exhibiting their works off the main road. **Café Bloom** *(Nottingham Road/on the R 103 | tel. 03 32 66 61 18 | Budget)* not only offers culinary delights; art lovers will also find something to their liking here. The owner Michael Haigh is an artist himself and makes pottery which he sells in the café; some of his works can even be bought at the Conran store in London. **Keep driving along the N 3 to the** ⑪ **Golden Gate Highlands National Park** → p. 70 in the Free State province. A good tip is to spend the night in the reserve at the **Highlands Mountain Retreat** *(tel. 01 24 28 91 11 | www.sanparks.org | Moderate)* where imposing sandstone cliffs shimmer golden in the sunlight.

After a long morning drive through the national park, **you will arrive at your next station along the R 712,** ⑫ **Clarens** → p. 70. Set aside enough time in this town to have a bite to eat and visit a few of the local galleries. Continue your journey to ⑬ **Ladybrand** → p. 71, a town on the border of Lesotho → p. 71, which is also known as the "kingdom of the sky". The **Cranberry Cottage** *(43 rooms | 37 Beeton Street | tel. 05 19 23 15 00 | www.cranberrycottage.co.za | Moderate)* is a well-located accommodation for the night.

The next day takes you on a drive along the R 701 through the Free State to the country's largest reservoir, the ⑭ **Gariep Dam.** The dam is popular with paragliders because of the perfect conditions *(www.gariepgliding.com)*. The area does not offer a wide selection of restaurants; the best is the **Mondrian** *(Aasvoel Street 2/at the Hotel De Stijl | tel. 05 17 54 00 60 | Expensive)*. **Drive on the R 390 towards** ⑮ **Cradock** → p. 37 where **Tuishuise** is a comfortable place to spend the night.

Head off the next morning to the **Mountain Zebra National Park** → p. 38 **and then on the N 9 to** ⑯ **Graaff-Reinet** → p. 36. The traditional **Pub Pioneers** *(3 Parsonage Street | tel. 04 98 92 60 59 | Budget)* serves excellent lamb dishes. Be-

Zebras in the national park

fore continuing on your journey, visit the **Valley of Desolation** with its impressive rock formations in the **Camdeboo National Park** → p. 37. **From the N 9 take a right turn onto the R 341 to ⑰ Oudtshoorn** → p. 36, the capital of the ostrich farming region. Live like an ostrich baron from the last century on the **La Plume Guest Farm** *(19 rooms | tel. 04 42 72 75 16 | www.laplume.co.za | Moderate)* where you can also sleep the night. Plan a day break here to visit at your leisure two ostrich farms, find out more about breeding ostriches and to sample scrambled eggs made with ostrich eggs for lunch.

Next, the **R 328** will take you over the **Schwartberg Pass**, one of the country's most impressive mountain passes, to ⑱ **Prince Albert**, a sleepy Karoo village with enchanting guesthouses. The **African Relish** *(34 Church Street | tel. 02 35 41 13 81 | www.africanrelish.com | Moderate)* not only offers lovingly furnished rooms but also cookery courses. If you do not have enough time, you should at least try the restaurant.

The next day starts **with a two-hour drive on the N 1, then turn left onto the R 318 and you'll reach** ⑲ **Montagu after a further 60 minutes.** The Cape's winelands start in this romantic village and it's worth parking up here for the day as there are lots of places to explore. Visit the hot **Avalon Springs** *(www.avalonsprings.co.za)*, take a mountain bike tour through the surrounding mountains or stroll around the historic centre. A stay at the **Mimosa Lodge** *(22 rooms | tel. 02 36 14 23 51 | www.mimosa.co.za | Moderate)* is a feast for the senses. The lodge and its elegant rooms are located in lovely gardens where you can hear the sounds of birds. The attached restaurant serves excellent cuisine and a very good house wine.

From Montagu take the R 60 via the wine town Worcester, until it veers left to the R 43. Continue on this route through Villiersdorp and past the Theewaterskloof reservoir to the Elephant Pass, with its spectacular view of the Franschhoek valley below. The wine town of ⑳ **Franschhoek** → p. 58 is right at the heart of the winelands to the east of Cape Town and is considered to be South Africa's culinary capital. Spend the night here and enjoy a relaxing dinner in one of the town's excellent restaurants.

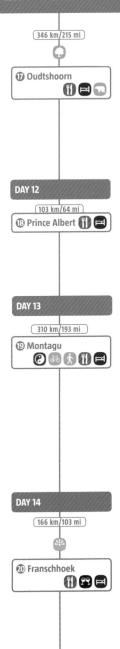

346 km / 215 mi

⑰ Oudtshoorn

DAY 12

103 km / 64 mi

⑱ Prince Albert

DAY 13

310 km / 193 mi

⑲ Montagu

DAY 14

166 km / 103 mi

⑳ Franschhoek

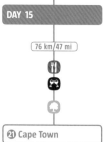

DAY 15

76 km/47 mi

㉑ Cape Town

On your last day the R 45 takes you past one wine estate after another. Just before you get to the motorway slip road in the direction of Cape Town you will come across one of the country's oldest wine estates: **Babylonstoren**. The vegetables and fruit prepared in the restaurant **Babel** *(Simondium Road | tel. 02 18 63 38 52 | Expensive)* are grown in the estate's spectacular gardens which you should definitely visit. **Continue on the N 1 for another half hour and you will finally reach** ㉑ **Cape Town → p. 51,** South Africa's oldest city.

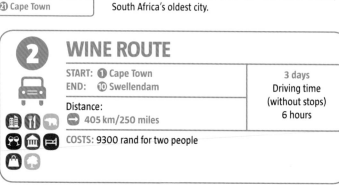

2 WINE ROUTE

START: ① Cape Town
END: ⑩ Swellendam

3 days
Driving time
(without stops)
6 hours

Distance:
➡ 405 km/250 miles

COSTS: 9300 rand for two people

This is an interesting trip even if you are already familiar with the well-known Cape wine estates. The drive begins in Cape Town and takes you along the Worcester and Robertson wine routes to the historic and interesting town of Swellendam and includes a boat trip, game drives and wine-tasting along the way.

DAY 1

① Cape Town

56 km/35 mi

② KWV Sensorium

45 km/28 mi

③ Du Toits Kloof Winery

22 km/13.6 mi

④ Worcester

Your journey starts in ① Cape Town → p. 51 and takes you on the N 1 to Paarl where it is worth visiting the ② KWV Sensorium *(57 Main Road | Mon–Fri 9am–4.30pm, Sat 9am–2pm)*, a combination of a fine art gallery and sophisticated wine-tasting establishment run by the region's largest producer of wine and spirits. **Continue along the same route and just before you reach the entrance to the Huguenot Tunnel exit the motorway and drive on the R 101 along the 70 km/43 mile-long and extremely picturesque Du Toits Kloof Pass. Once you arrive at the foot of the mountains, the road leads on to Rawsonville** where you can stop at the ③ Du Toits Kloof Winery *(www.dutoitskloof.co.za)* for a wine-tasting session. Aside from tasting excellent, the Chardonnay Viognier is cheap here too. **The R 101 takes you just outside** ④ **Worcester,** a town located in the centre of the country's biggest wine growing area. A fifth of the country's grapes are grown here which are made into wine by the local wineries. The **Kleinplasie Open Air Living Museum** *(Robertson Road | Mon–Fri 8am–4.30pm, Sat 8am–1pm | admission 15 rand)* just outside the town takes you back in time to the life of the early pioneers and farmers. The buildings are reconstructions of houses in the Cape region.

Now head north on the N1. After approximately 60 km/37 miles turn left onto the R 46 to Ceres and then it's just 4 km/2.5 miles to the entrance gate of the ⑤ **Aquila Private Game Reserve** *(33 rooms | tel. 02 14 30 72 60 | www.aquilasafari.com | Expensive)*. Home to Africa's Big Five, it is just under a two-hour drive from Cape Town and the ideal stop for visitors who do not plan to travel to the major game reserves. You can either spend the night in one of the comfortable chalets or just plan a day visit to the park.

The next morning sees you return to Worcester and then take the R 60 in the direction of Robertson. After 15 km/9.3 miles turn off left to ⑥ **Nuy.** Aside from the exceptional wines of the **Nuy Winery,** most of which are listed in South Africa's wine bible *Platter's,* Nuy also offers the eccentric **Nuy Valley** *(18 rooms | tel. 02 33 42 12 58 | www. nuyvallei.co.za | Budget)*. The guesthouse is worth a visit if

71 km/44 mi

⑤ Aquila Private Game Reserve

DAY 2

82 km/51 mi

⑥ Nuy

44 km/27 mi

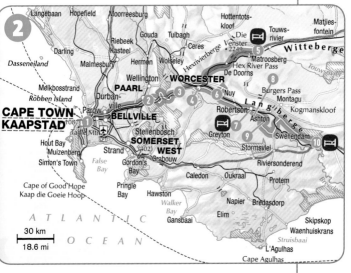

```
30 km
18.6 mi
```

Example of Wilhelminian architecture in Swellendam

only to see the VIP backpacker rooms in the old wine cellar. A few kilometres further along the R 60 is the start of the **Robertson Valley**, the valley of wine and roses. The first cooperative you encounter is INSIDER TIP **Rooiberg**, an insider tip for good, affordable wines. The best restaurant in ➐ **Robertson** is **The Small Restaurant** in the ultra-stylish **The Robertson Small Hotel** (*10 rooms | 58 Van Reenen Street | tel. 02 36 26 72 00 | www.therobertsonsmallhotel. com | Expensive*), which is perfect for your second overnight stay on this tour.

From Robertson, continue on the next day along the R 317. Some excellent wine estates are located along this side route. One particular recommendation is ➑ **Springfield** (*www.springfieldestate.com*). Aside from its excellent wines such as the Méthode Ancienne Cabernet Sauvignon, the wine estate is also popular with animal lovers as the estate's spacious grounds have been home to a herd of springboks for decades; with a bit of luck you'll be welcomed at the gate by antelopes who have escaped and are mischievously chewing on the grapes. The next estate is a unique experience for lovers of white wine. Danie de Wet, the owner of ➒ **De Wetshof** (*www.dewetshof.com*), is the king of the South African Chardonnay. His manor, which also houses the winery, reminds you more of a country estate in Tuscany than a South African farmhouse. **Get back**

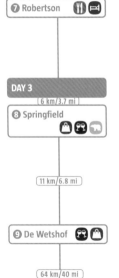

➐ Robertson

DAY 3

6 km/3.7 mi

➑ Springfield

11 km/6.8 mi

➒ De Wetshof

64 km/40 mi

onto the R 60 in Bonnievale and drive to ⑩ **Swellendam**, a charming town where you feel transported back to the early days of the first settlers. It is the third oldest settlement in the Cape and dates back to 1745; many of the historic buildings remind you of this period. The open air **Drosdy Museum** *(18 Swellengrebel Street | Mon–Fri 9am–4.45pm, Sat/Sun 10am–3.15pm | admission 35 rand)* is a showcase of buildings from the second half of the 18th century, one of which houses the **Field & Fork** restaurant *(26 Swellengrebel Street | tel. 02 85 14 34 30 | Moderate)* specialising in French cuisine. The small **Augusta de Mist** *(6 rooms | 3 Human Street | tel. 02 85 14 24 25 | www.augustademist.co.za | Expensive)* is perfect for an overnight stay before you continue on your journey along the Garden Route or return to Cape Town.

⑩ Swellendam

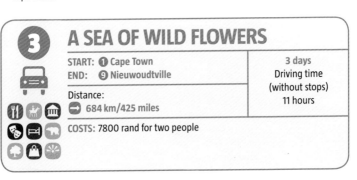

3 A SEA OF WILD FLOWERS

START: ① Cape Town END: ⑨ Nieuwoudtville	3 days Driving time (without stops) 11 hours
Distance: 🚗 684 km/425 miles	
COSTS: 7800 rand for two people	

Millions of wild flowers bloom in the Western Cape from August to October, transforming the area into a magnificent sea of colour. This floral show starts in Darling and stretches to Springbok in the Namaqualand; the most prolific flowers are the Namaqualand daisies. But the tour is also worth taking outside the flowering season.

From ① **Cape Town** → p. 51 take the N 7 north until you reach the Malmesbury exit. From there, head along the R 304 to ② **Darling**, a relatively sleepy village until 1995 when it was discovered by Pieter Dirk-Uys, South Africa's best satirist and performer who opened his own theatre in the old train station. During the apartheid era his alter ego Evita Bezuidenhout would cleverly mock the political issues of the day. The theatre is called **Evita se Perron** *(tel. 02 24 92 28 51 | www.evita.co.za | Budget)* which translates as "Evita's platform". Many other creative artists followed Pieter Dirk-Uys, turning Darling into a cultural hotspot. Enjoy lunch at **Darling Brew** *(48 Caledon Street | tel. 02 12 86 10 99 | Budg-*

DAY 1

① Cape Town

76 km/47 mi

② Darling

74 km/46 mi

_et_) where they brew their own beer. You need to book in advance if you would like to taste their beers.

The flowering landscape starts as soon as you leave Darling. **Take the R 307 and then the R 45 to Hopefield.** The **③ West Coast Fossil Park** (_Mon–Fri 9am–4pm, Sat/Sun 9am–1pm, guided tours every hour | admission 80 rand_) is located just after Hopefield and you can see 5 million year old fossils of animals there. Many species – such as bears or short-neck giraffes – have not inhabited this coastal region for many years. Head east to **④ Kersefontein** (_7 rooms | tel. 08 34 54 10 25 | www.kersefontein.co.za | Moderate_) which offers the perfect place for a stay over in a Cape Dutch manor house that has been in the hands of one family, the Melcks, for three hundred years. The owner Julian offers his guests horseback treks and sightseeing flights. In the evening, you can dine in 19th century style in the manor's dining room.

Heading north, the next stop is **⑤ Velddrif**. At the mouth of the Berg River on the Atlantic Ocean, this town has a spectacular setting and is a paradise for fishermen. If you prefer not to catch your own fish, then try the seafood and delicious fish dishes at **Sover-by Lapa** (_on the beach between Velddrif and Warskersbos | tel. 08 27 38 79 30 | Budget_), right on the beach. The town is famous for its sea salt products, the _Khoisan Natural Unrefined Sea Salt_ which is hand-harvested in enormous pans. The factory has a small **shop** (_5 Reservoir Road | www.khoisansalt.co.za_), which sells different types of sea salt. The bath crystals are particularly popular as they have a high mineral content to relieve pain and to detox. It's also worth an excursion to the romantic fishing village of **⑥ Paternoster → p. 46** just 30 km/19 miles away.

From Velddrif, the R 399 takes you back to the N 7. From there head further north to ⑦ Clanwilliam. Here in the Cedarberg is the country's centre for the production of rooibos tea and the only place in the world where the bush

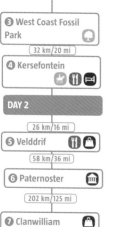

grows. If you would like to learn more, take a tour along the *Rooibos Route* (www.rooibos-route.co.za). **To reach your hotel for the night, leave Clanwiliam again and follow the signs to the ⑧ Bushmans Kloof Wilderness Reserve from the outskirts of town.** The route to this very unique natural reserve takes you 20 km/12 miles through dramatic mountain landscape. This private wildlife park at the heart of the Cedarberg Mountains is home to 140 species of birds and wild regional animals (from the mountain zebra to gemsbok and wildcats). It is also the site of more than 125 remarkable Khoisan rock paintings, mainly depicting animals and people. Enjoy a luxury overnight stay at the **Bushmans Kloof Wilderness Reserve & Wellness Retreat** (*16 rooms | tel. 02 14 37 92 78 | www.bushmans kloof.co.za | Expensive*).

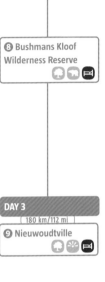

⑧ Bushmans Kloof Wilderness Reserve

DAY 3

180 km/112 mi

⑨ Nieuwoudtville

On the next morning **head back to Clanwilliam and from there approx. 80 km/50 miles along the N 7 to Vanrhysdorp. Take the exit to ⑨ Nieuwoudtville. The R 27 heads steeply uphill** and offers spectacular views of the Namaqualand flower splendour. A good accommodation for the night is **Swiss Villa** (*6 rooms | 116 Nassau Street | tel. 02 72 18 13 47 | www.nieuwoudtville.com/swiss-villa | Budget*), a guesthouse within a 100 year old sandstone villa. **Return to Cape Town the next day; the fastest way is on the N 7 which you can join at Vanrhynsdorp.**

Colourful wall paintings: the Khoisan drawings at Clanwilliam

BY BAZ BUS FROM JOHANNESBURG TO CAPE TOWN

START: ❶ Johannesburg **END:** ❿ Cape Town	10 days Driving time (without stops) approx. 46 hours

 Distance: 🔄 2623 km/1630 miles

COSTS: 12,500 rand per person
WHAT TO PACK: Most backpacker hostels provide bed linen but not towels.

IMPORTANT TIPS: The "Coast to Coast" guide is an essential travel companion. There are almost no ATM cash machines along the Wild Coast which is why you should take out enough money in Durban.

South Africa is the ideal travel destination for backpackers. The BAZ Bus is an uncomplicated means of travel and the country's backpacker lodges are among the best in the world.

The **BAZ Bus** running from Johannesburg to Cape Town *(4500 rand, return ticket 9000 rand | tel. 02 14 22 52 02 | www.bazbus.com)* is the perfect option for those who don't want to explore South Africa by car. The BAZ is a hop-on-hop-off bus; in other words you can get on and off as often as you wish on the booked route. It is a good idea to book your first backpacker hostel before you leave home. In ❶ **Johannesburg** → p. 82 the **Curiocity Backpackers** *(302 Fox Street | tel. 01 16 14 01 63 | www.curiocitybackpackers.com | Budget)* is a good place to start your tour. Guests can be collected from the airport and the BAZ provides all the information you need for travelling on the BAZ Bus, including the "Coast to Coast" *(www.coasttocoast.co.za)* guidebook which lists South Africa's best backpacker accommodation. There is always something going on in the recommended hostels. Guests share experiences and tips every evening over a beer. The BAZ Bus will often pick up passengers directly from their hostel's front door; remember to book your hostel a day in advance.

From Johannesburg, the first leg of the journey is to the ❷ **Drakensberg** → p. 79, the Alps of South Africa where **INSIDER TIP** **Amphitheatre Backpackers** *(tel. 08 28 55 97 67 | www.amphibackpackers.com | Budget)* on

DAY 1

❶ Johannesburg 🚍

DAY 2

317 km/197 mi

❷ Drakensberg

the outskirts of the **Royal Natal National Park** on the border to Lesotho offers excellent accommodation. The lodge has a wide range of activities to explore the Drakensberge Mountains. The night walks and abseiling courses are particularly recommended.

The route heads on to ③ Durban → p. 72, where you are obliged to stay the night as the bus takes a break here before continuing the next day. Located next to the uShaka Marine World, the **Happy Hippo** *(222 Mahatma Gandhi Road | tel. 03 13 68 71 81 | www.happyhippodurban.co.za | Budget)* is a good place to spend the day with a stroll to the Golden Mile beach promenade, a very busy destination in the evenings. For a small surcharge you can join the BAZ Bus on one of their city tours of Durban (as well, by the way, as in Port Elizabeth or Cape Town).

The next part of the journey takes you to the relatively undiscovered East Cape. Even so, the region has three of South Africa's most attractive backpacker hostels. **The Coffee Shack** *(tel. 04 75 75 20 48 | www. coffeeshack.co.za |*

DAY 3

270 km/168 mi

③ Durban

DAY 4

507 km/315 mi

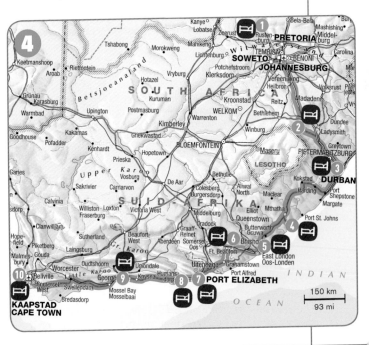

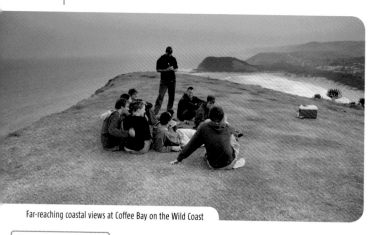
Far-reaching coastal views at Coffee Bay on the Wild Coast

4 Coffee Bay

Budget) in the isolated coastal town of **4 Coffee Bay** on the Wild Coast lies, as its name suggests, directly on the coast. You shouldn't miss out on two particular activities: a walk along the coast to the **Hole in the Wall** rock formation and the visit to a Sangoma, a traditional healer. The BAZ Bus does not take you directly to Coffee Bay **but there is a shuttle service from the Shell petrol station in Mthatha.**

DAY 5

310 km/192 mi

5 Chintsa

The route continues to **5 Chintsa** to the **Buccaneers** *(tel. 04 37 34 30 12 | www.cintsa.com | Budget)*. Chintsa is a small village and guests are housed in huts which are spread out over large grounds – a paradise for kite surfers and surfers.

DAY 6

172 km/107 mi

6 Hogsback

The next stop is the small town **6 Hogsback** → p. 38 with the backpacker lodge **Away with the Fairies** *(Bag End | Ambleside Close | tel. 04 59 62 10 31 | www.awaywiththefairies. co.za | Budget)* – a magical setting in a huge garden. A sundowner in the treehouse with beguiling views over the rain forest in the company of small monkeys is an amazing experience. The lodge also offers mountain bikes for active tourists – the owner is convinced that the country's best trails can be found here. The BAZ Bus is not direct; guests can be picked up from Buccaneers in Chintsa or from Sugarshack in East London.

DAY 7

263 km/163 mi

7 Port Elizabeth

An overnight stay in **7 Port Elizabeth** → p. 46 is mandatory because this is where the coach driver takes a break. **Lungile Backpackers** *(12 La Roche Drive | tel. 04 15 82 20 42 | www.lungilebackpackers.co.za | Budget)* offers something for travellers who are looking for action after days in the wilderness: the party mile in Humewood is in walking distance.

The next stop is another must, ❽ Jeffrey's Bay → p. 49, especially for passionate surfers looking for the perfect wave. The seafront accommodation at **Island Vibe** *(10 Dageraad Street | tel. 04 22 93 16 25 | www.islandvibe. co.za | Budget)* is a particularly appealing hostel.

Before the last leg of your journey to Cape Town, you should schedule a stop in one other town such as in ❾ Wilderness close to George → p. 33 along the Garden Route. The **Beach House Backpackers** *(Western Road | tel. 04 48 77 05 49 | www.wildernessbeachhouse.com | Budget)* is as nice as its name sounds. The house is located directly at the beach and the views are amazing.

From here it is only several more hours before you reach your destination, ❿ Cape Town → p. 51. The "Mother City" also has a wide choice of lodges for backpackers; one of the nicest is the **Atlantic Point Backpackers** *(2 Cavalcade Road | tel. 02 14 33 16 63 | www.atlanticpoint.co.za | Budget)* in Green Point, ideally located between the sea and the city..

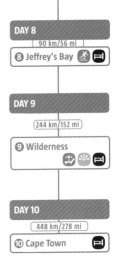

DAY 8

90 km/56 mi

❽ Jeffrey's Bay 🏃📷

DAY 9

244 km/152 mi

❾ Wilderness

DAY 10

448 km/278 mi

❿ Cape Town 📷

BY LUXURY TRAIN THROUGH SOUTH AFRICA
If you would like to travel in style through the Cape region then a train trip with *Rovos Rail (tel. 01 23 15 82 42 | www.rovosrail.com | prices per person depend on cabin category, approx. 20,200–40,500 rand)* is for you. If you do the Pretoria to Cape Town leg then you can look forward to 48 hours of creature comforts as you travel the 1600 km/994 miles through the breathtaking semidesert landscape of the Karoo. Travellers are welcomed to the station with a string quartet and a speech from its owner Rohan Vos. A historic locomotive pulls the train along the first section of the route. Guests meet in the lounge car, the observation car with large windows or in the dining car. The dress code is formal with a jacket and tie for dinner. The train stops for several hours during the night and pulls into *Kimberley (see p. 39)* at 10am the next morning where passengers can visit the *Big Hole and Kimberley Mine Museum.* The next stretch is along 700 km/435 miles through dramatic semidesert landscape. The next break is in Matjesfontein, a village founded in 1876 where you should visit the stylishly renovated *Lord Milner Hotel.* From here, the Rovos Rail travels through the fertile Cape with its wine estates and orchards and arrives at Cape Town main station at 6pm.

SPORTS & ACTIVITIES

Eternal summer. Well, ok, a very long summer at least. And a brief winter with spells of sunny and hot weather.

There is no reason to stay at home and most South Africans love the outdoor lifestyle and sports, taking both an active and passive pleasure in them. Typically, fitness studios are a hive of activity at five o'clock in the mornings.

BALLOONING

Like riding an escalator just with far better views. The only sporting prowess you need is when you climb into the basket. Starting from prices of 2000 rand upwards, *Bill Harrop's Original Balloon Safari (tel. 011 70 05 32 01 | www.balloon.co.za)* offers flights over the Magalies Mountains to the north of Johannesburg and the aerial equivalent of game drives above private wildlife reserves. *Suncatchers (tel. 08 78 06 20 79 | www.suncatchers.co.za)* offers the same in the Mpumalanga province close to the Drakensberg massif.

BUNGEE JUMPING

Daredevils are invited to do the world's highest bungee jump, more than 200 m (656 ft) off the Bloukrans Bridge near Plettenberg Bay *(tel. 04 22 81 14 58 | www.faceadrenalin.com)*. A more street-style alternative is to dive off the graffiti-sprayed Orlando Towers in Soweto *(tel. 07 16 74 43 43 | www.orlandotowers.co.za)*. Or why not try a freefall from the arc of the Moses Mabhida stadium?

Everything is possible in South Africa:
a relaxing game of golf, an exciting shark dive
or a ludicrously steep mountain bike cycle

Although technically speaking, it is more of a swing than a jump *(tel. 03 13 12 94 35 | www.bigrush.co.za)*.

CYCLING

It is not a good idea to cycle in the cities. Drivers simply do not expect to be sharing the road with anyone on two wheels and cycle lanes are only starting to appear – with the exception of Cape Town: racing bike cyclists are welcome here and many international racers spend their winter months training here. Cars become a minority in Cape Town once a year when the *Cape Town Cycle Tour* is held, the world's largest cycle race where thousands of cyclists compete to race around the Cape *(www.capetowncycle-tour.com)*. Bikes and tours are available at *AWOL Tours (tel. 02 14 18 38 03 | www.awoltours.co.za)* but if you are more interested in downhill racing then join a tour organised by INSIDER TIP *Downhill Adventures (tel. 02 14 22 03 88 | www.down-hilladventures.com)* on the Tafelberg.

You are treated to more views of the sea on tours along the Garden Route. Contact *African Bikers (tel. 02 14 88 30 00 | www. africanbikers.com)* for more information.

DIVING

Diving without sharks is also great, particularly in Sodwana Bay, close to the Mozambique border. The region is a marine reserve and the water temperature is not as cold as in False Bay near Cape Town for example. *Coral Divers (tel. 03 55 71 02 90 | www.coraldivers.co.za)* offers both equipment and courses. The Aliwal Shoal reef to the south of Durban is the remains of an ancient sand dune and divers can plunge to depths of 37 m/120 ft *(www.aliwalshoalscubadiving.com)*.

GOLF

In contrast to Europe, golf is seen as a national sport in South Africa, even if it is still dominated by whites. Green fees are not expensive and it is completely normal when a farmer heads off to his local golf club to unwind after a day at work. There are hundreds of courses, each one offering a splendid panorama. At *South African Tourism* (see p. 125) you can get the brochure *Golf in South Africa*. The most attractive golf resorts and hotels are: *Durban Country Club (www.durbancountry club.co.za)*, *Fancourt* on the Garden Route *(www.fancourt.co.za)* and *Arabella Hotel & Spa (www.mariott.com)* in Hermanus. Those who fancy a round should check out the website *www.lastminutegolf.co.za*.

KITESURFING

The introduction of new and improved equipment makes kitesurfing a little less dangerous than it once was. In Cape Town, the beach at Bloubergstrand or the Langebaan lagoon are perfect for the sport *(www.kitelab.co.za or www.*

Ideal for thrill seekers – a shark dive

constantlykiting.com). In Port Elizabeth: www.swingkiteboarding.com. Information: www.safarinow.com or www.kitesurfing.co.za. Find the Ocean to Air kitesurfing school on the beach in Durban (tel. 03 15 62 88 86 | www.ocean2air.com).

KLOOFING

Swimwear, hiking boots, helmet and sun cream are what you need to go kloofing. Admittedly, a harness and rope can be useful. This sport involves jumping over canyons and rocks, down waterfalls and up rivers. The Kamikaze Canyon is one of the most popular kloofs, meaning gorge or ravine in Afrikaans. Abseilafrica in Cape Town's Long Street offers day tours (www.abseilafrica.co.za). Kloofing in the Drakensberg Mountains is best done with Four Rivers Raftinig & Adventures (www.fourriversadventures.co.za).

MOUNTAIN BIKING

Possible all over South Africa. Each province has its own hot spots, even the bigger cities offer challenging trails and the more inland you venture, the more you'll feel like a modern-day voortrekker. Tony Cook Adventures (tel. 08 27 83 83 29 | www.mountainbikingafrica.co.za) along the Garden Route not only has its own trail park, the operator also organises day tours and bike holidays. One spectacular route is up (and down) the Drakensberg (www.alloutadventures.co.za).

SHARK DIVING

Anyone who has seen "Jaws" will find it difficult to imagine that humans are more of a danger to sharks than they are to us. Thankfully, responsible tour operators organise dives which ensure that the sharks are not disturbed. One op-

erator is Marine Dynamics Shark Tours (tel.07 99 30 96 94 | www.sharkwatchsa.com) in Gansbaai which organises shark cage diving trips to get up close and personal to a real-life shark for 1900 rand.

SURFING

South Africa is one of the few locations where the uncombed salt water look is appealing. The fantastic, awe-inspiring waves on the Atlantic and Indian Oceans are any surfer's paradise. The more hardcore junkies try their luck at the Dungeons in Hout Bay while those who value their lives head to Jeffrey's Bay on the Indian Ocean to pose in front of beginners at Jeffrey's Bay Surf School (tel.08 23 24 72 84 | www.jbaysurfschool.co.za). A day trip to the beach in Muizenberg is a must if you're based in Cape Town; most stores rent out surfing equipment such as www.lifestylesurfshop.co.za.

WELLNESS

The country's hotels and lodges offer many spas and treatments – you'll be reluctant to swap your bathrobe for your day clothes at the end of your stay. However since even smaller establishments also promise the perfect spa treatment, you are right to be choosy when deciding on where to go but expect to pay high prices. Beauty temples which combine relaxation with ancient African healing methods are definitely worth trying such as the INSIDERTIP Waters At Royal Malewane (www.royalmalewane.com) in the Kruger National Park. One of the nicest spas in KwaZulu-Natal is the Karkloof (www.karkloofsafarispa.com) near Pietermaritzburg. A treatment at the Twelve Apostles Hotel (www.12apostleshotel.com) in Cape Town will take your breath away – but only because of the hotel's sea view.

TRAVEL WITH KIDS

South Africa is a very child-friendly country, which could be because many of the families have more children than those in Europe.

Most restaurants have special children's menus, the waiters are generally very friendly to children and some restaurants even have crayons and colouring in books on hand. ICots and babysitting services are provided in hotels and guesthouses; some even offer children entertainment and clubs. To help set your mind at ease there are always lifeguards on duty at the popular beaches.

Children under 12 are not always welcome in certain boutique hotels or smaller guesthouses in very popular tourist areas around the Cape – however this information is usually highlighted on the website. Most owners simply don't want their delicately furnished houses to be tampered with or prefer to keep the noise down for their adult-paying guests. These establishments are an exception and children are generally very welcome.

CAPE PROVINCES

BIRDS OF EDEN
(135 E6) (*G8*)
This excellent free flight bird sanctuary also covers a section of indigenous forest. Many species of birds from all continents fly around freely in this 2 ha park. A *Monkeyland* and an enclosure for big cats are also in the vicinity. *www.birdsofeden. co.za | daily 8am–5pm | adults 230 rand, children 115 rand*

Amusement parks, game watching, boat rides: you will be spoilt for choice when it comes to fun things for the whole family to do

KWANDWE ECCA LODGE
(136 B5) (*ω J7*)
Located near Grahamstown, the lodge in the *Kwandwe Private Game Reserve* tailors to the needs of younger guests. Rangers are trained to show children the nature around. *6 suites | tel. 04 66 03 34 00 | www.kwandwe.com | Expensive*

INSIDER TIP PURE NATURE LODGE ⓥ
(136 A6) (*ω H7*)
Olaf and Marie Heidtke have made their wishes of a never-ending family holiday come true with their lodge with six individually furnished, spacious apartments at the Addo National Park. Besides the wilder animals, the lodge also has its own private farm with smaller creatures. Many breakfast ingredients are home-made and the lodge uses solar power. *Tel. 08 78 08 66 10 | www.pure-nature-lodge.com | Moderate*

OCEAN ADVENTURES (135 E6) (*ω G8*)
Boat trips from Plettenberg Bay to see whales, dolphins and seals up close. *Tel.*

04 45 33 50 83 | adults 500 rand, children 250 rand

CAPE TOWN AND SURROUNDS

DUIKER ISLAND (134 B6) (*Ⓜ D8*)
Boats ferry out from the small harbour in Hout Bay to Duiker Island, a breeding ground for seals. The glass bottom boat, the Calypso allows passengers to watch the comings and goings in the waters below. *Tel. 02 17 90 10 40 | www.circelaunches.co.za | adults 70 rand, children 40 rand*

INSIDER TIP **GLOWING ROOMS SA**
(134 B5) (*Ⓜ D8*)
Mini golf is always fun but when the course is lit up at night and is played using 3D glasses, you can expect to have a great time. *1 Turf Club Road | Milnerton | tel. 02 15 51 22 44 | www.glowingrooms.co.za | Tue–Thu 10am–7pm, Fri/Sat 10am–8pm, Sun 10am–3pm | admission 130 rand*

MONKEY TOWN (134 B5) (*Ⓜ D8*)
Spacious outdoor enclosures with 28 species of primates. The monkeys, all born in captivity elsewhere and held in inappropriate conditions, were rescued and brought here by various animal rescue organisations. *Somerset West | Cape Town | tel. 02 18 58 10 60 | www.monkeys.co.za | 9am–5pm daily | admission: adults 90 rand, children 55 rand*

PLANETARIUM (U A4) (*Ⓜ a4*)
A special show takes children on a journey through the secrets of the universe. *25 Queen Victoria Street | Cape Town | tel. 02 14 81 39 00 | www.iziko.org.za | adults 40 rand, children 20 rand*

SCRATCH PATCH (U F1–2) (*Ⓜ f1–2*)
Admittedly there are no real diamonds here, but children get to sit in giant trays filled with hundreds of thousands of semi-precious tumble-polished South African gemstones and „scratch" for their favourites. The small (or bigger) bags they fill are weighed and priced accordingly. *V & A Waterfront | Dock Road | tel. 02 14 19 94 29 | www.scratchpatch.co.za | daily 9am–6pm*

KWAZULU-NATAL

NATURAL SCIENCE MUSEUM
(137 E3) (*Ⓜ L5*)
This museum in Durban informs children of what they may be missed during their game drive through one of the reserves. Its collection of magnified insects is worth seeing. *234 Anton Lembede Street | Mon–Sat 8.30am–4pm, Sun 11am–4pm | admission free*

WAVEHOUSE (137 E3) (*Ⓜ L5*)
The amusement park in Umhlanga is a hive of activity with a wave pool, gigantic slides, sand pits and fun on wheels to entertain children. The staff looks after its younger guests while parents can sit back and relax. *In the Gateway Shopping Centre | tel. 03 15 84 94 00 | Mon–Fri 8.30am–5pm, Sat/Sun 8.30am–6pm | admission depending on activity 40–160 rand*

NORTHERN PROVINCES

INSIDER TIP **BAMBANANI**
(136 C4) (*Ⓜ J–K3*)
Childcare facilities are available at this attractive coffee shop in the Johannesburg district of Melville which has a huge courtyard for children to play, climb, run around and slide. Babysitting services and delicious meals are also available. The place gets busy at the weekends but is otherwise relaxed. *85 4th Av. | tel. 01 14 82 29 00 | www.bambanani.biz | Moderate*

GOLD REEF CITY AMUSEMENT PARK
(132 C4) (*m J3*)

More than 20 terrific rides will have your children queuing for more. The best attraction is a trip down a 200 m (656 ft) deep disused mine shaft where gold was once mined. *Johannesburg | M 1 south, Gold Reef City exit | tel. 0112485000 | www.tsogosun.com | daily 9.30am–5pm |*

es can be seen in action is here in Kyalami. The breed takes its name from the stud farm located in the village of Lipica in Slovenia. Midway between Johannesburg and Pretoria. *1 Dahlia Road | show Sun 10.30am | tel. 07 97 16 47 92 | admission 170 rand, children under 3 free*

Young herd boys at home in nature

admission 190 rand (inclusive of all the rides), family ticket 500 rand

JOHANNESBURG ZOO (132 C4) (*m J3*)
Johannesburg Zoo is home to more than 300 species of animals: those who missed the *Big Five* in the Kruger National Park can catch them in action here. Also night tours. *Parkview | www.jhbzoo. org.za | daily 8.30am–5.30pm | adults 80 rand, children 50 rand*

LIPIZZANERS (132 C4) (*m J3*)
One of the few remaining spots in the world where the white Lipizzaner hors-

INSIDER TIP VALLEY OF WAVES
(132 B3) (*m J3*)

If children could build a swimming pool in the jungle, it would surely resemble the waterpark in Sun City, northwest of Johannesburg. A 17 m/55 ft slide plunges you to the depths below and two-metre high waves appear every few minutes in the *Roaring Lagoon*. On a river you let inflatable tyres float you around the jungle; there is also a beach volleyball court. *Sun City | www.suninternatio nal.com/sun-city | May–Aug 10am–5pm, Sept–April 9am–6pm | adults 160, children 85 rand*

FESTIVALS & EVENTS

No matter what the occasion to celebrate, South Africans put their heart and soul into it. The diversity of cultures has brought with it a plethora of festivals and events. Approximately three quarters of all South Africans are Christians which is why Christmas and Easter are public holidays throughout the country.

FESTIVALS & EVENTS

JANUARY

Cape Town: *Kaapse Klopse*; Sstreet carnival held the day after New Year's Day in memory of the free day for slaves, the ancestors of today's *coloureds*. A vibrant, fun and loud event.

Cape Town: the country's most sophisticated and prestigious horse race the *Sun Met* is held at the *Kenilworth Race Course* on the last Sunday

MARCH/APRIL

Oudtshoorn: *Klein Karoo National Arts Festival* a cultural festival with theatrical productions and an art market at the end of March or beginning of April

Cape Town: with 30,000 participants the *Cape Town Cycle Tour* is the largest timed cycle event in the world, on the second Sunday in March

APRIL

Cape Town: national and international music buffs meet up for the *Cape Town International Jazz Festival* on the first weekend in April

JUNE

Pietermaritzburg and Durban: *Comrades Marathon*, annual ultra marathon, with 20,000 participants

JUNE/JULY

Grahamstown: *National Arts Festival* transforms the university town into an arts showcase for a fortnight from the last week in June to the first week in July

JULY

Knysna: the *Knysna Oyster Festival* where oysters are the focus for all the activities. Oyster-shucking and oyster eating competitions as well as sporting events. The first week in July

Franschhoek: *Bastille Day festival* on the Sunday closest to the 14th July. The wine estates, vintners and village restaurants get together to celebrate their French heritage with a wine and gourmet festival

Spectacular spring blossoms, music and dance: the vitality and variety of South Africa's festivals make them unique

AUGUST

Swaziland: The *Reed Dance* ceremony, known in Zulu as Umhlanga, is where 40,000 unmarried and childless Swazi girls holding long reeds perform a dance in front of the Royal Palace in Ludzidzini. As part of the ceremony, the women traditionally dance bare-breasted for their king who can then choose a new wife.

Cape Town: held in the second week, *Cape Town Fashion Week* showcases the country's designers

SEPTEMBER

Hermanus: held in the last week the *Whale Festival* celebrates the beautiful mammals that mate and give birth in the bay between June and November

OCTOBER

Pretoria: massive *Jacaranda Festival* with music, flea and farmers markets in the streets in the third week to pay tribute to the 70,000 trees that burst out in bloom

NOVEMBER

Cape Town: From the end of November to February th INSIDER TIP *Kirstenbosch Summer Sunset Concerts*; are held; great bands and super atmosphere in the Botanical Gardens.

NATIONAL HOLIDAYS

1 Jan	New Year's Day
21 March	Human Rights Day
27 April	Freedom Day
16 June	Youth Day
9 Aug	National Women's Day
24 Sept	Heritage Day
16 Dec	Day of Reconciliation

In the event of a public holiday falling on a Sunday the following Monday is a public holiday.

LINKS, BLOGS, APPS & MORE

LINKS & BLOGS

www.zar.co.za Contains a wealth of information about South Africa with statistics, history, trivia and biographies of famous South Africans like Nelson Mandela

www.sa-venues.com A site which will help you find accommodation even in the smallest town. Not necessarily all the establishments are listed but a small introduction is given to every town!

www.grape.co.za Tim James is a writer who has specialised in wine. His blog about the subject and the wine industry is an exciting read; he is also the co-editor and member of the jury for the *Platter's Wine Guide*

www.drizzleanddip.com The food and photography blogger Sam Linsell has posted a vast collection of food recipes and images of South Africa. It will get you drooling about the culinary delights awaiting you in the country

www.whatidranklastnight.co.za Wine connoisseur Christian Eedes' blog tag line is: "Good booze. Good food. Good company". His blog combines wit and knowledge to report on his favourite wines and his favourite restaurants

www.ecoatlas.co.za South Africa is way behind Europe in terms of sustainability and eco responsibility – the country was simply pre-occupied with other problems for a long time. The founders of this website are committed to helping consumers make the right decisions for the planet in all aspects of life. The website *www.greenpop.org* pursues a similar mission; they plant trees and environmental ideas in poor communities and make the occasion into a festival.

www.facebook.com On the Facebook page "I love Cape Town", more than 400,000 fans of the mother city talk about what's going on, where to go and what to do

www.inspiredlivingsa.co.za Fiona Rossiter from Cape Town writes about all that is beautiful in South Africa, from

Regardless of whether you are still prepaing your trip or already in South Africa: these addresses will provide you with more information, videos and networks to make your holiday even more enjoyable.

wine to restaurants to romantic getaways, recipes and fashion

www.twitter.com/gotosouthafrica official twitter account of South African Tourism. The latest news and insider tips on travel, sport and culture

www.yomzanzi.com this entertainment blog posts everything currently hitting the news in South Africa

VIDEOS & MUSIC

www.texxandthecity.com one of the country's best music journalists brings together young authors and contributors to the scene to present and rate local musicians

www.africam.com/wildlife live safaris are streamed online on this site. Animal waterholes are a popular recording spot in various wild parks. It almost feels like you are there

www.southafrica.info/video Worth checking out for the amazing travel videos that it showcases. Some also touch on the socio-political issues from an insider's view

APPS

Platter's Wine Guide The bible of South African wines and you can now load the app on to your mobile phone. Makes choosing the right wine a whole lot easier and more fun (www.wineonaplatter.com)

Eat Out A feast for foodies! Information on more than 5500 restaurants at your finger tips, with reviews by patrons and price comparisons. Free of charge. There is also a mobile site

Uber The private taxi service has successfully filled a niche in South Africa: quick, reliable tours from A to B. Perfect if you've enjoyed a few glasses of wine...

TRAVEL TIPS

ARRIVAL

O. R. Tambo International Airport outside Johannesburg is the major arrival point for international travellers. Most countries now offer regular direct flights to O. R. Tambo as well as to Cape Town International Airport. *South African Airways (www.flysaa.com)* has regular scheduled flights from major international cities. Some airlines regularly offer specials so it is worth taking a look other airlines like *British Airways (www.british-airways.com)* and *Emirates (www.emirates.com)*. The cheapest fares are in winter from end of April to end of June, the most popular (and expensive) are in summer from December to April. Book well in advance to avoid disappointment. Aside from SAA there are several other domestic airlines like *Mango (www.flymango.com)* and *Kulula (www.kulula.com)* for flights inside South Africa.

RESPONSIBLE TRAVEL

It doesn't take a lot to be environmentally friendly whilst travelling. Don't just think about your carbon footprint whilst flying to and from your holiday destination but also about how you can protect nature and culture abroad. As a tourist it is especially important to respect nature, look out for local products, cycle instead of driving, save water and much more. If you would like to find out more about eco-tourism please visit: *www.ecotourism.org*

BACKPACKERS

Accommodation options for backpackers in South Africa are excellent. Many hostels offer double rooms with private bathrooms in addition to dormitories. They are even good option for tourists travelling with a suitcase – considerably cheaper than a B & B. Get your free copy of the backpacker bible, *Coast to Coast* from any backpacker hostel *(www.coasttocoast.co.za)*.

BED & BREAKFAST

There is no shortage of Bed & Breakfast accommodation in South Africa. Often their owners are also well versed in assisting their guests with travel enquiries. For listings of top class B & Bs get the *Portfolio Collection* catalogue from any travel agency. *Central reservations tel. 02 12 50 00 15 | www.portfoliocollection.com*

BUS

The public transport systems of cities hosting the 2010 World Cup benefited greatly from the event. The most popular means of transport is the minibus taxi, a small bus which can transport up to 12–15 passengers. These small buses drive on all roads and will stop anywhere on request. The *REA VAYA (www.reavaya.org.za)* bus network has been launched in Johannesburg in recent years, which covers the journey from the city centre to Soweto. The shuttle service *MyCiti* is highly recommended for travelling around Cape Town. The means of payment is a *myconnect* card which can be purchased for 30 rand at the airport, ki-

From arrival to weather

Holiday from start to finish: the most important addresses and information for your trip to South Africa

osk or at a petrol station. You simply load money onto the card at ABSA Bank cash machines. More information available at *www.myciti.org.za*.

CAMPING

Its moderate climate makes South Africa an ideal destination for campers. Camping sites are found in all cities, on many beaches, in nature reserves and in conservation areas. Huts or bungalows are often offered to guests *(information: www.caravanparks.co.za)*. You can hire a camper van from rental companies like *Around About Car (www.aroundaboutcar.com)*.

CAR HIRE

Rental cars are less expensive in South Africa than they are in the UK. You can hire cars in all major cities but it is advisable to book a car in advance before travelling. The minimum age to hire a car varies so make inquiries beforehand. It is recommended to take out a full insurance coverage if you are planning to hire a car in South Africa. You can expect to pay around 2500 rand to hire a medium range car for a fortnight in peak season. The main car hire companies are *Avis (www.avis.co.za)*, *Budget (www.budget.co.za)* and *Hertz (www.hertz.co.za)*.

CONSULATES & EMBASSIES

BRITISH HIGH COMMISSION IN PRETORIA
255 Hill Street | Arcadia 0002 | Gauteng (Pretoria) | tel. 02 71 24 21 75 00 | uk insouthafrica.fco.gov.uk

Viewing platform on Table Mountain

BRITISH CONSULATE GENERAL IN CAPE TOWN
15th Floor, Norton Rose House | 8 Riebeeck Street | Cape Town 8001 | tel. 02 14 05 24 00

CANADIAN EMBASSY IN PRETORIA
1103 Arcadia Street | Hatfield (Pretoria) | tel. 02 71 24 22 30 00 | www.canadainternational.gc.ca/southafrica-afriquedusud

U.S. EMBASSY IN PRETORIA
877 Pretorius Street | Arcadia (Pretoria) | tel. 01 24 31 40 00 | za.usembassy.gov

U.S. CONSULATE GENERAL CAPE TOWN
2 Reddam Ave | Steenberg, 7945 | tel. 02 72 17 02 73 00 | za.usembassy.gov/embassy-consulates/capetown

CUSTOMS

Among others the following goods can be imported duty-free to South Africa:

BUDGETING

Kruger Nat. Park	£16/$21.50 *admission*
Coffee	£1.35/$1.80 *per cup*
Cola	£0.60/$0.77 *per standard can*
Petrol	approx. £0.82/$1.08 *per litre*
Sunscreen	£4.50/$6 *a tube*
Steak	£8.20/$10.80 *for 300 g*

CURRENCY CONVERTER

£	ZAR	ZAR	£
1	17	10	0.60
3	50	30	1.80
5	84	50	3
13	218	130	7.80
40	670	400	23.90
75	1260	750	44.80
120	2010	1200	72
250	4200	2500	149
500	8400	5000	298

$	ZAR	ZAR	$
1	13	10	0.80
3	39	30	2.30
5	65	50	3.80
13	169	130	10
40	520	400	31
75	975	750	58
120	1560	1200	92
250	3250	2500	192
500	6500	5000	385

For current exchange rates see www.xe.com

1 L spirits, 200 cigarettes and goods not exceeding 5000 rand in value. The following goods can be imported duty-free into the EU: 1 L spirits, 200 cigarettes and goods not exceeding 400 pounds in value. Do not take a risk by exporting protected plant and animal species or their products. It is strictly prohibited. By the same token the import of seeds and plants is also not permitted. For more information go to *south-africa.visahq.com/customs*

DRIVING

Third party insurance to cover passenger liability is compulsory for anyone driving a vehicle in South Africa. Car rental companies include this in their rates. The speed limit in towns and cities is 60km/h, on provincial routes 100km/h and on the motorway 120km/h. Fines for speeding can be exorbitant. You drive on the left hand side of the road. The blood alcohol limit is 0.05%.

Around 168,000 km of road is surfaced, another 367,000 km is not. Some motorways are toll roads, like the one that links Johannesburg and Durban and almost the entire distance from Johannesburg to the Kruger National Park. These routes are demarcated with a white T on a blue background and you can pay by credit card. The South African traffic rules governing a four-way stop can be confusing for tourists. Whoever arrives at the intersection first drives off first. If two cars arrive at the same time, drivers use hand signs to agree who drives off first. The Automobile Association of South Africa (AA) is represented throughout the country.

ELECTRICITY

220 Volt/50 cycles per second. Three pronged plugs are the norm so you may

require an adapter. Hotels will generally be able to provide one and they can also be found in most supermarkets.

EMERGENCY SERVICES

Police: *10111*
Ambulance and fire brigade: *10177*
Tourist crisis incident reporting: *08 31 23 23 45*

HEALTH

Visitors to the Kruger National Park and to the Limpopo, Mpumalanga and Natal nature reserves and adjoining areas are advised to take malaria prophylaxis. You can buy malaria tablets without a prescription in any chemist in the country and need only start the course on arrival in South Africa. No inoculations needed. Found in all the cities and larger towns, South Africa's privately run hospitals are state-of-the-art and their healthcare world class. NHS or government health insurance certificates from other countries are not accepted here. It is imperative that you take out appropriate travel insurance.

IMMIGRATION

Visitors entering South Africa must be in possession of a valid passport and visitors from the UK, EU, USA, Australia and New Zealand do not require a visa for a stay of 90 days or less. Passports must be valid for six months and should have at least two unused pages. For children under 18 years of age, you'll have to submit an international birth certificate. Should the child be acompanied by only one custodial parent, you must also show a declaration of consent as well as a certified passport copy of the absent parent.

INFORMATION

SOUTH AFRICAN TOURISM UK
2nd Floor, 1-2 Castle Lane, London SW1E 6DR. Call centre 020 8971 9350 | uk.southafrica.net

SOUTH AFRICAN TOURISM USA
500 5th Avenue 22th Floor, Suite 2200, New York NY 10110. Call centre 1 800 593 1318 | www.southafrica.net/usa

GENERAL INFORMATION: *www.brand southafrica.com* and *www.sa-venues.com*

ADDITIONAL INFORMATION: accommodation: *www.portfoliocollection.com;* events bookings: *online.computicket.com/web;* game parks: *www.sanparks.org*

INTERNET & WIFI

WiFi and Internet access can cause surprises in South Africa. Most hotels and guesthouses provide internet access as a standard service, yet it is not always certain that you will get a good connection, if at all. A similar problem is encountered with the cost: it belongs to the customer service in some hotels, restaurants and coffee shops while others charge extortionate prices. It is advisable to buy a local SIM card and data package because the mobile internet connection is usually good.

MONEY, BANKS & CREDIT CARDS

The currency is the rand. It can be up to 20 per cent cheaper to exchange money in South Africa itself. You can withdraw cash using your Visa, MasterCard or debit card at most ATMs. Bank opening times: Mon–Fri 9am–3.30pm, Sat 9am–11am. Banks sometimes close for lunch in smaller towns. All credit cards are accepted and are the common methods of payment even for smaller purchases. You can encounter problems when paying by Mastercard but Visa always works.

OPENING TIMES

Stores in South Africa are generally open from Monday to Friday 9am to 5pm and 9am to 1pm on Saturdays. Some larger shopping centres are open seven days a week until 5pm on Saturdays and 1pm Sundays. The V & A Waterfront in Cape Town is open 365 days a year from 9am to 9pm.

POST

Postcards to Europe cost 7.25 rand to send and a letter weighing up to 10g 8.40 rand. Do not forget to affix an air mail label. Post can take from five to 14 days to arrive. Opening times: *Mon–Fri 8am–4.30pm, Sat 8am–noon.*

PHONE & MOBILE PHONE

You will always dial ten digits to m call locally; land line numbers all in the city code. You can hire SIM cards mobile phone operators (*Vodacom,* *Cell C*) at the airports and then to card up with credit. If it proves to ficult to register at the airport, tr smaller electric kiosks in the major which are often operated by India Pakistanis and offer a pre-registere Card. You can buy phone credits a permarkets and petrol stations. The for phoning overseas is 00 follow the country code, e.g. UK 0044, US Canada 001, Australia 0061. The co calling South Africa is 0027.

SAFARI

There are game reserves for every and budget. The state-run game res

WEATHER IN JOHANNESBURG

	Jan	Feb	March	April	May	June	July	Aug	Sept	Oct	Nov
Daytime temperatures in °C/°F	26/79	25/77	24/75	22/72	19/66	17/63	17/63	20/68	23/73	25/77	25/77
Nighttime temperatures in °C/°F	15/59	14/57	13/55	10/50	6/43	4/39	4/39	6/43	9/48	12/54	13/55
Sunshine hours/day	8	8	7	8	9	9	9	10	9	9	9
Precipitation days/month	13	9	8	7	3	1	0	1	2	8	11

Surfers at Durban looking for the perfect wave

are good value for money (*Budget–Moderate*) but are best booked a year in advance: *National Parks (tel. 01 24 28 91 11 | reservations@parks.org)*. KwaZulu-Natal administers the state-run nature reserves within its borders separately to the aforementioned *(tel. 03 38 45 10 00 | www.kznwildlife.com)*.

There is an enormous choice of excursions available to the South African wilderness. It is therefore a good idea to decide what you want to see beforehand. A few recommendations. Big Five: *Kruger National Park* or *Madikwe Game Reserve*. Elephants: *Addo Elephant National Park*. Flora: *West Coast National Park*. Landscape: G*olden Gate Highlands National Park*. In KwaZulu-Natal (KZN), the Big Five can be spotted in the *Hluhluwe-iMfolozi Park* and fans of hippos should head to the *iSimangaliso Wetland Park*.

The best time to visit a game reserve is during the South African winter (April to September). In the rainy summer season the game is not drawn to the best observation spots, the watering holes. The lush vegetation also means less visibility.

TAX REFUND

You are eligible to be refunded 14 per cent VAT on a purchase of 250 rand or more, provided you can present a tax invoice. For purchases over 5000 rand, you are obliged to provide your name and address. The items together with the bills are presented at the airport, the latter being stamped and the refunded amount is then recorded in the *VAT Refund Office*. It can take weeks before the amount is reimbursed. Plan enough time and inform yourself of the procedure beforehand: *www.taxrefunds.co.za*.

TIME

South Africa is on Central African Time (CAT) which is one hour ahead of the UK during the South African summer and two hours during the South African winter.

TIPPING

It is common practice to leave a tip of between 10 and 15 per cent of the total. This is especially the case in restaurants. In South Africa your bill does not include the waiter's gratuity – at least in most cases. In the larger cities and tourist area some restaurants now add a 10 per cent service charge on to the bill so it is a good idea is to read the small print.

ROAD ATLAS

The green line indicates the Discovery Tour "South Africa at a glance"
The blue line indicates the other Discovery Tours

All tours are also marked on the pull-out map

Photo: Road leading through the Drakensberg mountains

Exploring South Africa

The map on the back cover shows how the area has been sub-divided

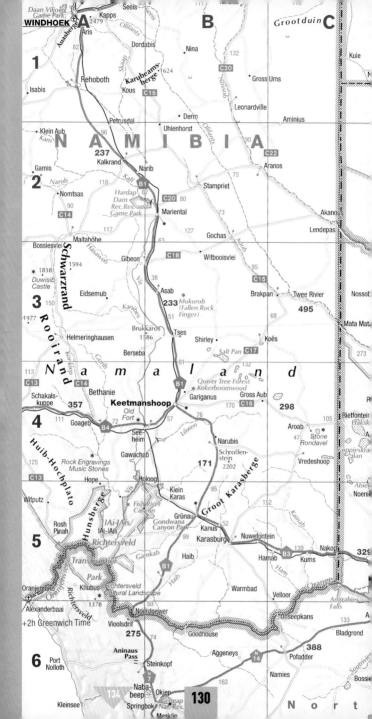

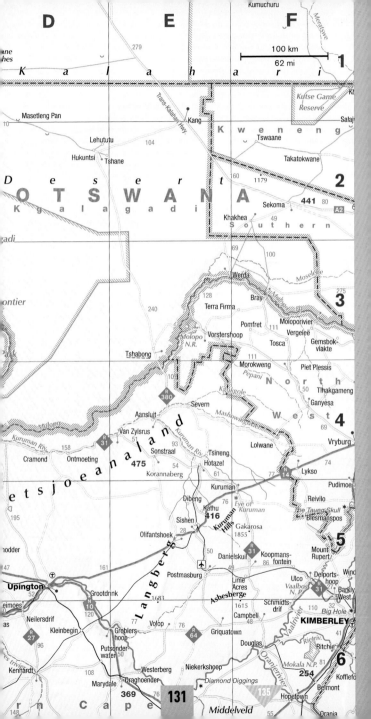

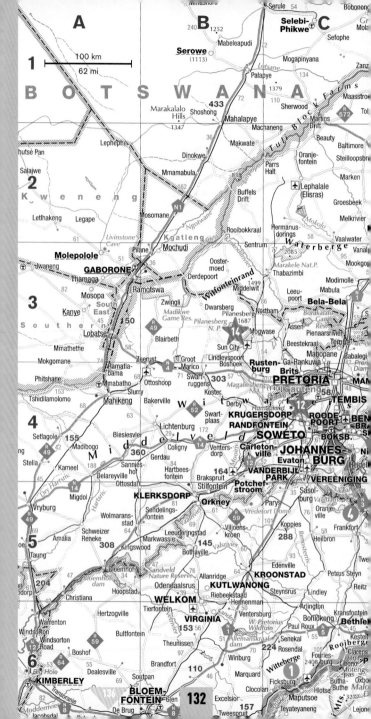

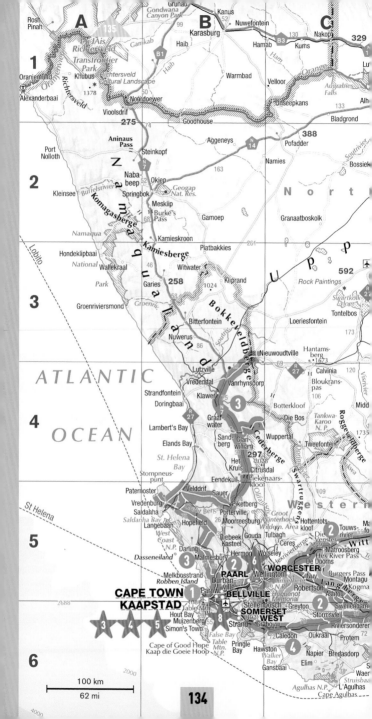

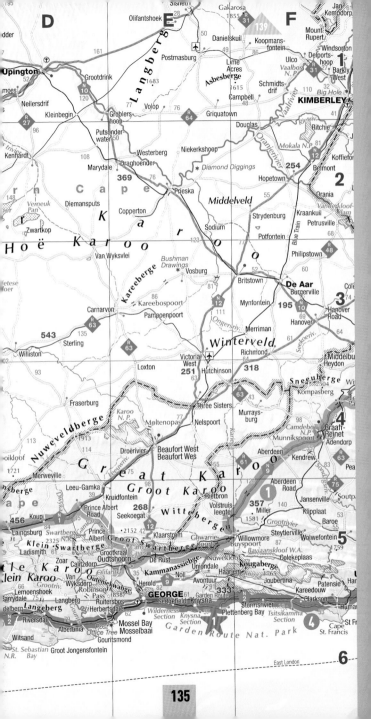

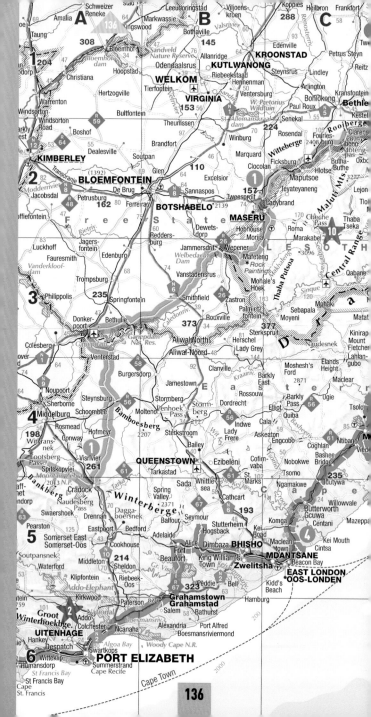

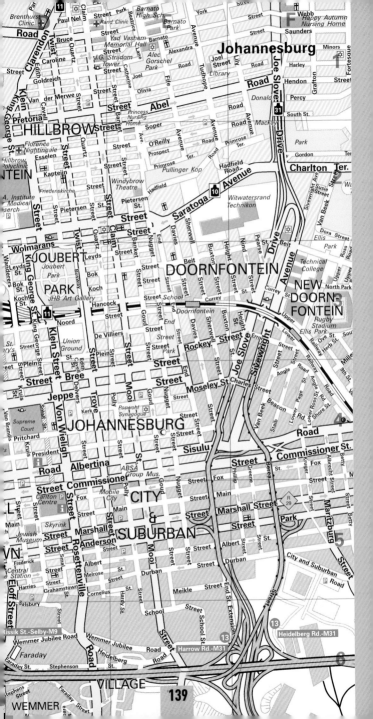

Autobahn, mehrspurige Straße - in Bau Highway, multilane divided road - under construction	═══ ═ ═ ═ ═	Autoroute, route à plusieurs voies - en construction Autosnelweg, weg met meer rijstroken - in aanleg
Fernverkehrsstraße - in Bau Trunk road - under construction		Route à grande circulation - en construction Weg voor interlokaal verkeer - in aanleg
Hauptstraße Principal highway		Route principale Hoofdweg
Nebenstraße Secondary road		Route secondaire Overige verharde wegen
Fahrweg, Piste Practicable road, track		Chemin carrossable, piste Weg, piste
Straßennummerierung Road numbering	B2 C 33 R 521 N 1	Numérotage des routes Wegnummering
Entfernungen in Kilometer Distances in kilometers	259 130 \ 129	Distances en kilomètres Afstand in kilometers
Höhe in Meter - Pass Height in meters - Pass	1365	Altitude en mètres - Col Hoogte in meters - Pas
Eisenbahn - Eisenbahnfähre Railway - Railway ferry		Chemin de fer - Ferry-boat Spoorweg - Spoorpont
Autofähre - Schifffahrtslinie Car ferry - Shipping route		Bac autos - Ligne maritime Autoveer - Scheepvaartlijn
Wichtiger internationaler Flughafen - Flughafen Major international airport - Airport	✈ ✈	Aéroport importante international - Aéroport Belangrijke internationale luchthaven - Luchthaven
Internationale Grenze - Provinzgrenze International boundary - Province boundary		Frontière internationale - Limite de Province Internationale grens - Provinciale grens
Unbestimmte Grenze Undefined boundary		Frontière d'Etat non définie Rijksgrens onbepaalt
Zeitzonengrenze Time zone boundary	-4h Greenwich Time -3h Greenwich Time	Limite de fuseau horaire Tijdzone-grens
Hauptstadt eines souveränen Staates National capital	**AL-QĀHIRA**	Capitale nationale Hoofdstad van een souvereine staat
Hauptstadt eines Bundesstaates Federal capital	**BULAWAYO**	Capitale d'un état fédéral Hoofdstad van een deelstat
Sperrgebiet Restricted area		Zone interdite Verboden gebied
Nationalpark National park		Parc national Nationaal park
Antikes Baudenkmal Ancient monument	∴	Monument antiques Antiek monument
Sehenswertes Kulturdenkmal Interesting cultural monument	Rock ✳ Paintings	Monument culturel interéssant Bezienswaardig cultuurmonument
Sehenswertes Naturdenkmal Interesting natural monument	Sudwala ✳ Caves	Monument naturel interéssant Bezienswaardig natuurmonument
Brunnen Well		Puits Bron
MARCO POLO Erlebnistour 1 MARCO POLO Discovery Tour 1		MARCO POLO Tour d'aventure 1 MARCO POLO Avontuurlijke Routes 1
MARCO POLO Erlebnistouren MARCO POLO Discovery Tours		MARCO POLO Tours d'aventure MARCO POLO Avontuurlijke Routes
MARCO POLO Highlight	★	MARCO POLO Highlight

MARCO POLO TRAVEL GUIDES

The travel guides with
Insider
Tips

INDEX

This index lists all places and sights, plus the names of important people and key words featured in this guide. Numbers in bold indicate a main entry. N.P. = National Park

CREDITS

WRITE TO US

e-mail: info@marcopologuides.co.uk

Did you have a great holiday?
Is there something on your mind?
Whatever it is, let us know!
Whether you want to praise, alert us
to errors or give us a personal tip –
MARCO POLO would be pleased to
hear from you.
We do everything we can to provide the
very latest information for your trip.

Nevertheless, despite all of our authors'
thorough research, errors can creep
in. MARCO POLO does not accept any
liability for this. Please contact us by
e-mail or post.

MARCO POLO Travel Publishing Ltd
Pinewood, Chineham Business Park
Crockford Lane, Chineham
Basingstoke, Hampshire RG24 8AL
United Kingdom

PICTURE CREDITS
Cover photograph: Elephant in the Addo Elephant Park (Schapowalow)
Photos: Norman Catherine (18 centre); Gettyimages: M. Dormer (87), B. Krist (63); Gettyimages/Lonely Planet (19 top); Gettyimages/ManoAfrica (74); huber-images: J. Foulkes (54/55), Huber (4 top, 50/51), G. Simeone (118/119); Laif: Emmler (117, 118), M. Gumm (44, 57), C. Heeb (66/67, 72/73), P. Hirth (32/33), Huber (127), T. Linkel (25), H. Meyer (119), O. Oberholzer (flap right); Laif/ Le Figaro Magazine: Fautre (77); Laif/GAMMA-RAPHO: D. & S. Balfour (91); Laif/hemis.fr: P. Frilet (43), F. Guiziou (36), R. Mattes (76, 92/93); Laif/Le Figaro Magazine: Frances (14/15); Laif/robertharding: P. Groenendijk (102), Y. Levy (59); Look: H. Holler (18 bottom, 20/21, 29); Look/Minden Pictures (40/41); Look/Photononstop (30/31, 80/81, 120 top); mauritius images/Alamy: P. Titmuss (60); mauritius images/Africa Media Online (22); mauritius images/age fotostock: B. Harrington (82); mauritius images/age fotostock/GFC Collection (34); mauritius images/Alamy (2, 3, 7, 9, 10, 11, 28 right, 52, 84, 94/95, 105, 112, 120 bottom), G. du Preez (68), G. B. Evans (70), B. Gibbons (98), M. Sobreira (19 bottom), K. Sriskandan (6, 123); mauritius images/Axiom/Remsberg (4 bottom, 26/27); mauritius images/cgimanufaktur (64); mauritius images/Cultura/Flipside (18 top); mauritius images/Cultura/Studio CP (114/115); mauritius images/Firstlight (108); mauritius images/Food and Drink (28 left); mauritius images/iconotec (31); mauritius images/imagebroker: D. Bleyer (39, 89), M. Graben (12/13), N. Overy (30), J. & C. Sohns (49); mauritius images/imagebroker/White Star: R. i Kubo (flap left); mauritius images/Juice Images (5, 110/111); mauritius images/nature picture library: G. Eaton (8); mauritius images/robertharding: I. Trower (47); H. Mielke (121); Schapowalow (1)

2ⁿᵈ edition – fully revised and updated 2018
Worldwide Distribution: Marco Polo Travel Publishing Ltd, Pinewood, Chineham Business Park, Crockford Lane, Basingstoke, Hampshire RG24 8AL, United Kingdom. Email: sales@marcopolouk.com
© MAIRDUMONT GmbH & Co. KG, Ostfildern
Chief editor: Marion Zorn; Author: Dagmar Schumacher, Co-author: Kerstin Welter; Editor: Jochen Schürmann; Programme supervision: Lucas Forst-Gill, Johanna Jiranek, Nikolai Michaelis, Kristin Wittemann, Tim Wohlbold; Picture editor: Gabriele Forst, Stefanie Wiese
What's hot: Kerstin Welter and wunder media, Munich; Cartography road atlas & pull-out map: © MAIRDUMONT, Ostfildern; Design cover, p. 1, cover pull-out map: Karl Anders – Büro für Visual Stories, Hamburg; interior: milchhof : atelier, Berlin; p. 2/3, Discovery Tours: Susan Chaaban, Dip.-Des. (FH)
Translated from German by Neil Williamson; Susan Jones
Prepress: writehouse, Cologne; InterMedia, Ratingen
Phrase book in cooperation with Ernst Klett Sprachen GmbH, Stuttgart, ditorial by Pons Wörterbücher

MIX
Paper from responsible sources
FSC® C124385

DOS & DON'TS ✌

A few things you should bear in mind in South Africa

DON'T DRIVE TOO FAST ON THE MOTORWAY

Overseas tourists may find it inconceivable that pedestrians and animals will cross the motorway. In South Africa it is quite commonplace so drivers should be cautious and aware. It is also not an uncommon sight to see horses, cattle and sheep grazing on the grass verges of motorways.

DON'T ROLL DOWN YOUR CAR WINDOW

Beggars are a common sight at many traffic lights. Do not open your car window to give them money – this would only increase the begging. Food, on the other hand, might help. Don't let anyone see the bags or mobile phones you have in your car.

DON'T FEED THE ANIMALS

As a rule the feeding of animals is prohibited in all game parks. Even the baboons that roam freely alongside roads and near rest spots should not be fed. Sadly they have completely lost their fear of man and when a car stops they will not hesitate to climb on the roof. If you dare open a car door they will be inside in no time scrounging for food and will eat everything and anything edible or not that they can lay their hands on. Many a woman's handbag – with passport, papers and all – has fallen into the hands of these primate thieves.

DO BE WARY OF GIVING SOMEONE A RIDE

With public transport being erratic in some areas it is not an uncommon sight to see people hitchhiking. They will be picked up by other willing locals in no time. Tourists on the other hand should exercise caution and avoid picking up hitchhikers. It will be impossible for you to gauge whether it is safe to give someone a ride.

DON'T TRUST ZEBRA CROSSINGS

As disciplined as South Africans are when it comes to queuing up, discipline goes right out the door when it comes to how they behave in traffic. The cardinal rule is that as a pedestrian you cannot go by the assumption that the driver of a vehicle will stop for you just because you are about to cross a street at a zebra crossing. On the other hand, if you are behind the wheel, never go by the assumption that pedestrians will stop at a red traffic light – the saving grace is that you can be sure that cars will stop at a red light!